Windows Containers for IT Pros

Transitioning Existing Applications to Containers for On-premises, Cloud, or Hybrid

Vinicius Ramos Apolinario

Apress®

Windows Containers for IT Pros: Transitioning Existing Applications to Containers for On-premises, Cloud, or Hybrid

Vinicius Ramos Apolinario
Newcastle, WA, USA

ISBN-13 (pbk): 978-1-4842-6685-4 ISBN-13 (electronic): 978-1-4842-6686-1
https://doi.org/10.1007/978-1-4842-6686-1

Managing Director, Apress Media LLC: Welmoed Spahr
Acquisitions Editor: Joan Murray
Development Editor: Laura Berendson
Coordinating Editor: Jill Balzano

Cover image designed by Freepik (www.freepik.com)

Distributed to the book trade worldwide by Springer Science+Business Media LLC, 1 New York Plaza, Suite 4600, New York, NY 10004. Phone 1-800-SPRINGER, fax (201) 348-4505, e-mail orders-ny@springer-sbm. com, or visit www.springeronline.com. Apress Media, LLC is a California LLC and the sole member (owner) is Springer Science + Business Media Finance Inc (SSBM Finance Inc). SSBM Finance Inc is a **Delaware** corporation.

For information on translations, please e-mail booktranslations@springernature.com; for reprint, paperback, or audio rights, please e-mail bookpermissions@springernature.com.

Apress titles may be purchased in bulk for academic, corporate, or promotional use. eBook versions and licenses are also available for most titles. For more information, reference our Print and eBook Bulk Sales web page at http://www.apress.com/bulk-sales.

Any source code or other supplementary material referenced by the author in this book is available to readers on GitHub via the book's product page, located at www.apress.com/9781484266854. For more detailed information, please visit http://www.apress.com/source-code.

Printed on acid-free paper

To my wife, Marcia, who during the writing of this book gave me the best present ever: our baby girl, Julia! Thank you for your support, always! Love you!

Table of Contents

About the Author

Vinicius Ramos Apolinario is a Senior Program Manager on the Windows Container platform team at Microsoft – the team that builds the container platform that runs on Windows Server and Azure. He has been a Microsoft professional for most of his career and holds multiple certifications from Microsoft, VMware, EXIN, and others. Vinicius is passionate about passing on his knowledge and contributes to the community via blogs, events, and articles. He is a published author who is regularly seen out in the community or at trade events presenting on various topics.

About the Technical Reviewer

Thomas Maurer works as a Senior Cloud Advocate at Microsoft. He engages with the community and customers around the world to share his knowledge and collect feedback to improve the Azure cloud platform. Prior to joining the Azure engineering team (Cloud + AI), Thomas was a Lead Architect and Microsoft MVP, to help architect, implement, and promote Microsoft cloud technology.

If you want to know more about Thomas, check out his blog (www.thomasmaurer.ch) and Twitter (www.twitter.com/thomasmaurer).

Acknowledgments

I'd like to first thank my wife Marcia for the amazing support throughout the process of writing this book. I accepted this project knowing she was pregnant and knowing I was not gonna be able to finish it before the baby arrived – and even with that she, as always, supported me and incentivized me to go ahead with it.

I also want to thank my manager at Microsoft – Taylor – who also supported me in this process, even with the crazy amount of work we all have at Microsoft.

Introduction

Have you ever looked into technical resources about how containers work and ended up on a Visual Studio Code demonstration? Well, that's because most of the content out there is focused on the developer audience. That doesn't mean IT Pros don't have a role here. In fact, running the infrastructure that supports containers, managing containers, and ensuring they run correctly and are properly managed are still important aspects that IT Pros play a part in.

This book is focused on the admins out there that are seeing the rise of containers and have Windows applications and infrastructure they need to support. How to transition to Windows containers? How to get started with it? What is Docker and Kubernetes? How can I use Azure to run containers? These are all questions that we will answer in this book.

We'll start from the basics so you can get a lay of the land – what containers are, what Docker is and how it works on Windows, and what the architecture of containers looks like on Windows and how it compares to regular virtual machines. Then we dive into how to use containers and Docker commands. From starting your first simple containers with nothing in them to more complex examples, we'll walk you through the process and explain what everything is and how it works in detail.

We then get serious with containers by moving existing applications into Windows containers and cover how to manage them once they are deployed. We cover how to interact with containers; how to manage devices, storage, and networking; and more. We then show how Windows Admin Center can be used to make some tasks easier in a friendly user interface.

Finally, we cover how to use Azure services to run your containers – Azure VMs, Azure Container Registry, Azure Container Instances, App Service, and Azure Kubernetes Service – so you can not only understand how Windows containers work but also feel confident to take on a new project and deploy your workloads in production using Windows containers!

CHAPTER 1

Introduction to containers

Let me tell you a story:

John is an IT admin currently working for a medium company. He has been managing physical hosts and virtual machines (VMs) for a long time – even before joining this company. John has worked with Active Directory, mail servers such as Microsoft Exchange, file servers, and many other infrastructure and networking components. One thing he learned over the years is the importance of keeping servers with the right configuration and only approved software installed. This has saved him in the past in audits and performance measurements, but also in keeping servers secure. Recently, John was put in a project alongside a development team to build a new module for their enterprise resource planning (ERP) system. His role in this project? Ensure servers are up and running with high availability (HA) and the new module is running as expected. After a couple weeks of meetings, development, and testing by the development and quality assurance (QA) teams, John has been handed the first version of the new module, along with a Word document describing how to deploy it. John follows the instructions on the Word doc – how to configure the operating system (OS), folder structure, and network and then, finally, install the .exe file. After installing, John sees a new icon on the desktop, which he then opens – and guess what? One of the services in the application fails. Is this story familiar to you? Has that ever occurred to you? If the answer is yes, this book is for you.

Where containers started?

When you hear about containers today, you will hear about many positive characteristics: they start faster, they allow for a better approach on DevOps practices, they have small footprint compared to VMs, and so on. However, the reason containers were created was to solve one fundamental problem in the IT industry – which is exactly the preceding scenario with John. In theory, applications should work the same way

© Vinicius Ramos Apolinario 2021
V. Ramos Apolinario, *Windows Containers for IT Pros*, https://doi.org/10.1007/978-1-4842-6686-1_1

regardless of where they are deployed. In the preceding story, can you find out what is wrong and why the application did not work? If John followed all the steps in the document provided by the development team, why did the application fail? In the majority of the cases, the answer is there was some application requirement missing. It might be that John missed one step from the document, or it might be the developer forgot to add one step to the document. In some cases, it might be even because the development environment had a bunch of other software installed on which the application depended upon and the developer never noticed. This situation is more common than it sounds.

In a nutshell, a container is a packaging of the application along with all other related requirements for that application to work. When running, a container has its own isolated view of the file system and registry, and that is not only isolated from the host but also from other containers. That means an application inside the container will always perform the same way. As you will learn in this book, containers are much more than that, but you should never forget why they were created in the first place. Funny fact: The reason why this technology received the name "containers" is because the nature of shipping containers is mostly the same. In the past, shipping companies found themselves in a difficult situation when they started to get orders of all kinds of goods to be shipped across the globe. To solve that problem, the industry created a standard shipping container size on which any type of good can be put in on one side and delivered on the other – with one standard for the shipping container and for the vessel transporting it.

Although containers really took off in the past few years, the technology to enable it has been around for a long time. Linux has had this technology for a long time, and even Microsoft has investigated it in the past. However, this technology only started to be adopted when Docker came in and connected a few dots. We will look in more detail on what Docker is later, but here are the main things they did to make containers successful:

- A standard for creating and packaging container images as well as pulling and pushing it (we will explain more about images later in this chapter)

- A specification for the container runtime so different OS could run the same container image standard via one API entry point

- An open repository for container images on which users could push and pull images to and from

  - A container runtime that works on different OS allowing developers
    to write the application once and have it run the same way on differ-
    ent environments

In 2015, Docker took another step that was extremely important to the adoption and growth of the container ecosystem by establishing the Open Container Initiative (OCI). This initiative brought together many other developers and companies interested in creating an ecosystem of services for companies interested in running their applications on containers. You can find more information on the OCI at their website: www. opencontainers.org/.

If we look at the IT landscape today, containers are the foundation and enablers of much of what has been developed today: DevOps technology, Serverless, Cloud computing, and so much more. If you were to ask me "Can you summarize containers in one paragraph?", this would be it: containers allow developers to package an application and its dependencies in one standard on which you can deploy it and have the application executing and behaving the same way regardless on where you deploy it. In addition, because they have a small form factor and you don't have to boot an entire OS, containers offer better performance when compared to VMs. Finally, they allow for better DevOps practices since you can reuse the same recipe for creating container images with the instructions on how to build the application.

With all that, there's still one issue that hasn't really been addressed by the market yet: containers (and all tooling around them) have been created by developers for developers, and most of the tools out there are focused on Linux and open source. In this book, I intend to give you an overview of Windows containers from the infrastructure and operations perspective – someone like John. Although we might need to explain a few developer-related topics, we will cover what containers are with the eyes of someone not focused on the code. So, let's dive into that!

How are containers different from VMs?

You might be thinking that some of the benefits I described earlier are also true for VMs and wondering why containers are so special. In fact, applications packaged in a VM will (almost) always perform the same way – they have their own view of the file system and registry. In fact, VMs are completely isolated from host and other VMs and even have their own kernel. Well, that's exactly the problem with VMs. When you spin up a VM, the VM itself "thinks" it is running on a dedicated hardware with its own processor, memory,

3

disk, networking, and so on. And it runs its own OS with its own kernel. In terms of isolation, that is a high standard. In terms of management, not so much.

The "problem" with VMs is that you have to manage each VM as an individual instance. Thinking about each VM instance, you have to install an OS, update it, back it up, and configure its settings to then start configuring your application. And managing a VM is a constant exercise. In contrast, containers offer a more streamlined approach to how the application is instantiated. A container doesn't have a dedicated OS – instead, it shares the same kernel from its container host. The isolation I mentioned before is then achieved by a combination of techniques. Each OS (Linux and Windows) implements this in a different way, but this method is called process isolation.

Process isolation means the container will be on a layer above the kernel. This layer above the kernel is usually referenced as user mode. Containers have their isolated user mode and consequently their own view of the file system and registry.

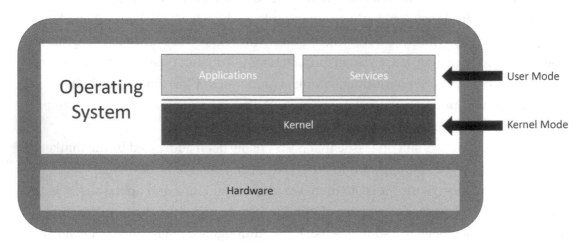

Figure 1-1. *Traditional deployment*

In Figure 1-1, we have the applications being deployed on user mode, and the kernel is responsible for scheduling hardware access (along with many other attributions, of course). When you deploy a VM, you are virtualizing everything above the hardware. A new partition is created for the VM, thus achieving isolation, but with a full-blown deployment. If you think about it, it's actually ironic that VMs are being replaced by containers since VMs were created to provide a better hardware utilization.

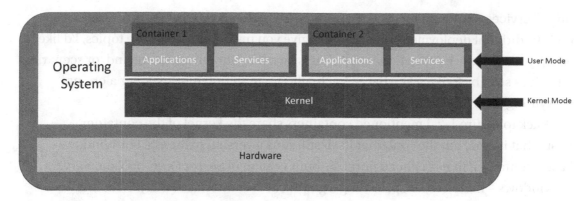

Figure 1-2. *Containerized deployment*

In Figure 1-2, we have two applications deployed, each one in its own container. You can see that we're still running the application in user mode and we're still with one single kernel. However, now each application has its own boundary with process isolation – the container itself. Here are a few things to call out:

- – If something happens to Container 1, Container 2 will continue to work without any interruption.

- – Both Containers 1 and 2 share the same kernel, but they have their own view of the file system and registry. If a file is added to C:\ AppFolder in Container 1, Container 2 won't see that. In fact, not even the host will see that.

- – Although both containers have their own view of the file system and registry, they still need the kernel on the host to run processes. Because of that, the process on both Containers 1 and 2 are visible from the host. (We will explore isolation and what the host can see from each container in more detail later in this chapter.)

It all sounds great, and at this point, you are probably thinking "I should run containers for my workloads." Well, it's not that simple.

When to use containers and when to use VMs

Let me open this chapter by telling you there is no definitive answer to that question. In fact, still today there is a lot of debate in the IT industry around which workloads should or should not be running in containers, if the best architecture for applications is microservices or monolithic, and if companies should adopt DevOps practices or keep their traditional deployments. Rather than give you my opinion on these topics, I'd like to equip you with the information to do what is best for your environment and/or scenario. First, let's start by looking at what can actually run in a container – spoiler alert, not everything runs in a container.

Back to Figure 1-2, I mentioned containers share the kernel of the container host. That is true, but the container itself still runs a version of the OS. For Windows-based container, that is either a purpose-built version of Server Core, or Nano Server, or Windows – none of them providing a graphical user interface (GUI). With that information alone, you can probably guess that applications relying on any GUI application programing interface (API) will fail. But it's more than that. The Server Core version, for example, is not the same OS you can install in a physical machine or VM. This image was tailor-made to run on containers and does not provide all the infrastructure roles and features that you are used to. For example, Active Directory, DNS, DHCP, and many other roles are not available to be installed. In fact, you can check which roles and features are not available on containers by running the following command:

```
Get-WindowsFeature | Where-Object {$_.InstallState -eq "Removed"}
```

The preceding command takes us to the next question: if there is no GUI present in containers, how do I interact with them? Keep in mind that interacting and managing a container are two different things. Interacting means running the container and executing commands in it. Managing it means checking its state, performance, and so on. We will cover management later in Chapters 4 and 5. As for interacting with Windows Containers, you would do that via PowerShell. Command Prompt is also available, but PowerShell ends up being the preferred way most people will interact with Windows containers. However, it's important to make one crucial distinction here. As an IT Admin, you are used to logging into a server/VM or remote connecting to it via a Remote Desktop Protocol (RDP). When doing that, you interact with the server/VM to perform whatever action, such as checking logs, operating the server/VM, and so on. In the containers' world, it's not expected that you interact directly with a container instance. Rather, the container should start with the desired state and configuration already in place. If something needs to be adjusted, you bring the container instance down, reconfigure the image from which the container is created, and then spin up a new instance. This approach is probably the main differentiation for IT admins moving from VMs to Containers and is usually referred to as "cloud mindset." In the next section, we will explore an approach to running resources that is crucial to containers: defining a desired state to resources via script or code.

Going back to how we manage VMs, here's the process you have probably used to prepare a VM for later use: You go to Hyper-V Manager (or vCenter – whatever platform you're using), and you start the process of creating a new VM. Then you specify the VM hardware – processor, memory, networking, disk, and so on. You then start the VM and either boot from a virtual disk or from the network to start the Windows installation process. You configure Windows regularly and install any application, and when you're done, you run a famous process called "Sysprep." Sysprep is a native tool in Windows used to generalize the current installation so it can be used for new installations. Usually after running Sysprep, you turn the VM off and discard the VM configuration files, preserving its virtual disk only. This virtual disk can then be used to create new VMs without running into a situation on which you have duplicated server names or any other unique identifier. From there, the process can be fully automated, and spinning up new VMs can be completed using automation rules with PowerShell or any other tool. With containers, we do it completely different.

Earlier in this chapter, I mentioned one of Docker's contributions was to create a standard for creating and packaging container images. What that means is that containers are created based on a template called container image. Those container images are not created by spinning up a new container instance and then generalizing it like VMs. Instead, container images are created based on a recipe that describes how the template (or container image) should be created. We will explore more how this works in the next section.

Finally, just like the GUI APIs, other APIs have been removed from the OS images available. Most of these APIs have been removed to reduce the footprint of Windows containers. The side effect is that this means regular applications might not run at all simply because they can't interact with the OS itself. Unfortunately, to answer the question if an application can be containerized or not, you will have to try to run the application and check for yourself. We will cover more details on how to containerize existing applications in Chapter 3. All of the described in the preceding paragraphs is considering a Server Core–based container. While not the same as a regular Server Core, it is still an option for containerizing existing applications, particularly applications running in .Net Framework. For new applications based on .Net Core, Nano Server is a better option as it provides support for it. However, Nano Server has its API surface further reduced, allowing only applications specifically developed to it.

To close on making a decision on when to use containers or VMs, the next thing you need to know about containers is that they are "stateless" in nature. What that means is that containers were not supposed to store state. To explain this concept, think about a self-contained application – an application that only requires a VM instance to run. Everything is stored in the VM. If you turn off the VM, the application stops, but if you turn the VM back on, the application will start work again. That seems obvious but is only possible because the storage of the VM is persistent. If the VM were to lose its content every time it powered off, it would be a nightmare, right? Well, yes, but that presents other issues. How do you scale a web application, for example, if all the data is contained in one single VM? The way to do that is by segregating your application into tiers. Traditionally, to achieve that in a web application, you would have at least two tiers: web tier and data tier. The web tier is the one dealing with the user requests and in the Windows world would be running an Internet Information Service (IIS) instance. VMs in this tier would have stateless versions of the applications that can receive user requests and query or write to the data tier. Scaling this web tier requires that you bring new VMs and add them to a Network Load Balancer (NLB). Because these VM instances are stateless, you can add and remove VM instances to satisfy the requests as you wish – as long as the NLB can probe these instances and know who is up and who is not. For the data tier, you would be running a database (DB) that is responsible for persistently storing the data. There are many DB products in the market, and it's not the goal of this book to go into much detail here, but let's say we're using Microsoft's SQL Server. SQL Server allows you to have multiple SQL Server instances to support large-scale deployments by offering multiple options for high availability (HA) and data replication. Different from the web tier, the db tier is stateful – if a server goes down, the data written into its DB is not accessible and could cause an application to either malfunction or in some cases even lose data, hence the need for techniques for HA and replication.

That's a lot. I know. What all that has to do with containers, you might ask. Containers were created with the stateless mindset. We will explore more on storage for containers in Chapter 4, but for now, what you should know is that, as mentioned earlier, when a container needs to be brought up, it is not bringing any data with it. If persistent data needs to be provided, it needs to be stored separately from the container.

To clarify, let's look at the following comparison Table 1-1:

Table 1-1. *Containers and VM comparison*

Feature	VM	Windows containers
Kernel	Has its own kernel	Shares underlying container host kernel
OS	Any supported OS	Existing base container images only
OS APIs	Full OS APIs	Limited set of OS APIs
State	Stateful	Stateless
Boot	Slow – dependent on VM OS	Fast – OS components already on underlying container host OS
Portability	Limited – dependent on hypervisor and other hardware components	Highly portable – dependent only on container host supporting the container OS and version
Graphical user interface	Supported	Not supported

As mentioned at the beginning of this section, there's no definitive answer for when to use containers and when to use VMs. With time, you will have a better understanding of key scenarios where each option provides more benefits. Running a large monolithic application? You should probably keep running it in a VM. Running a web application? You should try running it in a container. Want to modernize an existing application? Containers might or might not work, honestly. Your development team is working on a new application? Well, they should probably consider containers. Note that all my answers to the preceding questions are not definitive.

Before we move on to the next section, I want to make sure you understand that this chapter is focused on defining key concepts that will help you understand what containers are, when to use them, how to use them, and so on. As explained earlier, the way you interact with containers is through the docker toolset via PowerShell. While in the next sections we will show some of these commands, keep in mind that these will be explored in more detail in the following chapters.

What are container images?

In the previous section, we talked about container images and how they serve as a template for new containers. Now it's time to look at how container images work.

As mentioned previously, container images are templates from which new containers will be created from. For a container to run, we need a base OS, an application runtime, and the application itself – not much different from a VM, right? The main difference is on how we build container images. As mentioned, container images are built from a standard introduced by Docker. This standard is expressed in a text file called "dockerfile" (yes, this is a text file called dockerfile like that, no extension). To facilitate the understanding of it moving forward, I will reference it as docker file when talking about the concept of it and dockerfile when referencing it as a file in examples.

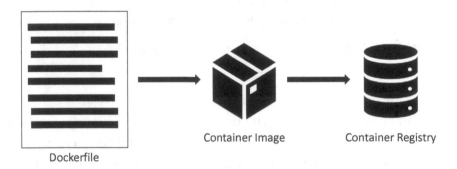

Dockerfile   Container Image   Container Registry

Figure 1-3. *Container image creation process*

As can be seen in Figure 1-3, the first thing you need to do to create a container image is to write a docker file with the specification of your application. Docker can read that specification and build a new container image with the instructions inside the docker file and store that new container image in your own container host. From there, you can run new containers based on that image but limited to that container host. If you want other container hosts to be able to run containers based on this container image you just created, you should upload it to a location on which other container hosts can download it. These locations are called container registries. Remember the things Docker did to make containers more usable? The Docker Hub was another one of those. We're going to cover container registries in more detail in the next section.

There is a big advantage of having containers being created this way – rather than manually configuring each container. Let's go back to the VM world and imagine a scenario in which you created a VM template for your application by hand, that is, create a VM, install the OS, configure the OS, install a runtime, install the application, configure the application and any other necessary step, and then generalize the image with Sysprep. A couple weeks after you deployed that version of the application into multiple VM instances, your dev team alerts you that a new version of the application is available. You'd have to repeat the preceding process all over again. With containers and the docker file, all you have to do is point the instructions on the docker file to the new version of the application and build a new version of the container image. For best practices, you should also create a new docker file for that specific version of the application so you can keep track of all changes.

One other interesting aspect of container images is that they are built in layers. When building a container image, Docker will read the instruction on the docker file and execute the commands in each line one at a time. Each execution creates a new layer for the container image. When a container host requests a container image from a registry, Docker will analyze the layers already present in the container host and only download the necessary layers. This process is called "pull" and greatly simplifies and accelerates spinning up new containers.

To make an analogy between container images and how you deploy VMs, let's go back to the example earlier of creating a VM template. Think of a docker file as a place where you write the instructions on how to deploy your web app. If you had to write it down, you would probably have something like this:

- Step 1: Start from a fresh installation of Windows Server 2019.

- Step 2: Install the IIS role and all the necessary sub-components.

- Step 3: Copy the web application folder from the source location to the VM instance.

- Step 4: Create a new web application on IIS pointing to the folder you copied on the previous step.

- Step 5: Generalize VM image with Sysprep and save the virtual disk for reuse.

Voilá! You now have all the instructions to deploy your web application. Now let's take a look at an example of a docker file:

```
FROM mcr.microsoft.com/windows/servercore/iis:windowsservercore-ltsc2019
WORKDIR /inetpub/wwwroot
COPY . .
```

At this point, you can probably guess what the preceding code means, but looking at it for the first time can be a bit overwhelming. Let's dig into what each of these lines mean.

Every docker file starts with the command "FROM". This instruction indicates what your base container image is. A base container image is an image that has the minimum for you to get started on deploying your application inside this container. A base container image can be any container image on Docker Hub, on your container host, or any other repository that you have access. Usually, you will want to work with a base container image that has the framework you want to use and was built by a trusted source. For example, if you want to run a website, you can use an official version of an IIS image produced by Microsoft. If you want to run an ASP.Net website, there's another image available from Microsoft specifically for that. There are hundreds of thousands of images available out there with a multitude of frameworks and tools, so you don't have to start from scratch. With that said, on the Windows side of containers, you should be aware that every container image (and consequently, every container) is built from three base images:

- Server Core: As explained in the previous section, this OS image is based on the Server Core installation option of Windows Server and provides a good set of APIs, including .Net Framework. This image is most often used for scenarios on which you want to containerize an existing application. Because it provides a large set of APIs and system components, this image is relatively large, especially when compared to standard Linux containers. As of the writing of this book, the Server Core container image from Windows Server, version 1903, has 1.92GB. After pulled, the image uses 4.63GB on disk. However, Microsoft has recently (as of writing) announced a reduction of 40% in size on the Server Core base container image for its next release of Windows Server – to be released in the first half of 2020. This new reduction results in an image of 1.13GB that uses 2.63GB on the disk.

- Nano Server: While the preceding reduction is impressive, it is still way too big when compared with Linux images that are only a few MBs in size. The answer to that is the Nano Server base container image. This image is 98MB in size and uses approximately only 251MB on disk, which is pretty impressive for a Windows instance. Of course, that comes with a price: not all APIs are available on the Nano Server base container image. In fact, not even .Net Framework is available – only .Net Core. You can still install other frameworks like Java, NodeJS, and others, but still not everything will work. Also, applications need to be developed targeting these frameworks on Nano Server, which means this will only work with new projects.

- Windows: This base container image is focused on scenarios where you need a broader set of Windows APIs. One example of what has been recently added to this image is DirectX support, allowing scenarios where you need access to this framework for applications that are GPU dependent. Like that, there is a whole set of other APIs added to the image, making it the larger in the Windows family of base container images with 5.72GB in size and 8.07GB on disk.

Back to our docker file, after the FROM command, you see that we are calling mcr. microsoft.com/windows/servercore/iis:windowsservercore-ltsc2019. This represents the registry on which the image is stored, the image itself, and the image tag. Let's break it down to better understand each part of it:

- mcr.microsoft.com: This is the registry on which Microsoft stores its official container images. MCR stands for Microsoft Container Registry. MCR is a deployment of Azure Container Registry (ACR) used by Microsoft. We will cover MCR and how you can create your own registry on ACR in future chapters.

- windows/servercore/iis: This is the image you are targeting to be deployed. Microsoft has Linux and Windows images available so the naming convention to distinguish Windows images starts with Windows, followed by the base OS image explained earlier – Server Core – and then IIS, which is the server role we are looking for. This specific image naming is very intuitive. You can clearly see that all

Microsoft did was to take a Windows deployment of Server Core and enabled IIS on top of it. In fact, if you look at the Docker Hub page of this image, you can even see the docker file Microsoft used to build the image.

– windowsservercore-ltsc2019: This is the image tag. Under the image explained in the previous bullet point, Microsoft could create differ-ent tags to represent different versions of the same image. For exam-ple, there could be a tag for Semi-Annual Channel (SAC) releases, a tag for specific monthly updates, and so on. It's important to note that when you are creating an image, if you don't specify a tag, Docker will tag your image as "latest". While this convention was useful in the past, it has been less used nowadays to avoid using an image you were not expecting. Today, the best practice is to always specify the tag of the exact image you want to use.

So with the FROM line explained, what Docker will do is to spin up a container, run the command in that line, save the container as an image, discard the temporary container, and move to the next line.

The WORKDIR command establishes the working directory on which the following commands and executions will happen. It's important to note here that for traditional Windows administration can be a bit confusing here. That's because Windows usually uses a full path to describe a location, such as C:\Inetput\wwwroot or %windir%\ system32. For the docker file, you can use that, but you will also find multiple examples of usage of context. Context in this case means the folder you are currently situated for command-line usage. For example, when you open the Command Prompt (CMD), by default, you are in the context of C:\users\[username]. Whatever command you execute will be executed in this "context," so if you need to execute a command against a file in another folder, you need to change the context or call out the full path of that file. For the dockerfile, there are two important contexts: the context of where you build your image on your container host and context of the commands you execute inside the temporary containers used to build your image. The first one (context for the container host) will be determined by the folder on which you execute the docker command to build the container image – we'll cover that in a minute. The second one, by default, is the C:\ drive. Setting the WORKDIR parameter inside the docker file helps you specify the folder on which you want to execute commands, copy files, and so on. In the preceding example, our working directory is C:\inetpub\wwwroot, but you see that we did not have to specify the C:\ drive. Also, you'll notice we use slash or forward slash "/" instead of backslash "\". This is just a notation standard in the docker file.

Finally, we are using the parameter COPY to specify which files we want to copy from the container host to the container image. At first, seeing two dots as in our example ". ." is a bit confusing. However, now that you understand "context," it's easy to see what we mean here. Basically, what we are telling docker to do is to copy the content from the host – represented by the first dot – to the container image, represented by the second dot. The reason we used a dot is because we don't want to hard-code the information for that command in the docker file. So when the docker command to build a new container image is executed, docker will copy using the context of the container host (first dot) to the container working directory (second dot).

That's it. We now have a docker file ready to be used to build a new container image. We will explore the command-line interface (CLI) for Docker in more detail in the next chapter, but for now, what you have to know is that most of the interaction with the container runtime (docker) is made via CLI. With that said, here is the next step to finalize building our container image:

- I have saved the website content in a folder under C:\MyWebSite.

- I have saved a dockerfile in the same preceding folder.

- Using an elevated session of Command Prompt, we navigate to the preceding folder and run the following command:

```
PS C:\MyWebsite> docker build -t mycontainerimage:v1 .
```

The output of the preceding command will be

```
Sending build context to Docker daemon  2.048kB
Step 1/3 : FROM mcr.microsoft.com/windows/servercore/iis:windowsservercore-
ltsc2019
 ---> 1dfea62c25d8
Step 2/3 : WORKDIR /inetpub/wwwroot
 ---> Running in 6d87a0a99ebb
Removing intermediate container 6d87a0a99ebb
 ---> cdbecca03030
Step 3/3 : COPY . .
 ---> 1a9b0b32ea7f
```

```
Successfully built 1a9b0b32ea7f
Successfully tagged mycontainerimage:v1
```

From the preceding output, you can clearly see the concepts we covered in this section. Each line containing a command was executed in sequence in a temporary container. That temporary container was used to execute the action for that command and saved as a layer, and then at the end, all temporary containers were discarded, and the layers formed our newly created container image. One important aspect here is that since we built our container image from the Server Core image with IIS, any other container host with that image already stored will only need to pull the specific layers for this image, instead of pulling all layers again.

To realize the advantage of this model, let's explore what happens if a new version of the application is made available.

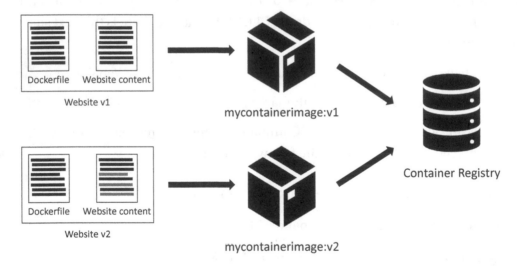

Figure 1-4. *Container image versioning*

The beauty of using a model such as the docker file is that the process of building a new image doesn't change from version 1 to version 2. In fact, as shown in Figure 1-4, you can copy the docker file used to build the container image v1 and store it in the new folder with the version 2 of the application and re-run the preceding command – just changing the v1 parameter to v2 so you can differentiate one image to the other. In a DevOps scenario, this is great as now you can

- Consistently reproduce your container images when you have a new version of the application.

- Reduce manual errors automating the building process.

- Spin up a new version of the application and, if something goes wrong, quickly come back to the previous version.

To check the container images in your container host, you can run the following command:

```
PS C:\> docker images
```

This command will return a list of images stored in your container host. Here's an example output:

```
REPOSITORY          TAG         IMAGE ID        CREATED         SIZE
Mycontainerimage    v1      1dfea62c25d8    3 hours ago     5.15GB
Mycontainerimage    v2      1a9b0b32ea7f    2 hours ago     5.16GB
```

What are container registries?

In the previous section, we explored what a container image is and how they are built. An image stored in a container host, however, can only be used in that specific container host. To make this container image available for other hosts, we need a central location to store images that can be used by other container hosts – either in your company or anywhere else if you so choose. These central locations are called container registries.

The most famous container registry is the Docker Hub (http://hub.docker.com) on which thousands of companies and users share their container images for usage by others. Of course, you can make a registry strictly available to you or your company. Docker offers free repositories for individuals who want to publish container images with the public and paid versions for individuals and companies who'd like to limit the access to their images.

Just like Docker, many other companies offer cloud services to host container registries. This is possible because these container registries follow the OCI standard. Here are some of the main companies offering container registries:

- Microsoft: `https://azure.microsoft.com/en-us/services/container-registry/`

- Amazon: `https://aws.amazon.com/ecr/`

- Google: `https://cloud.google.com/container-registry/`

- IBM: `www.ibm.com/cloud/container-registry`

These companies will offer different services and functionalities depending on your subscription and agreement. Some will not only store your container images but also integrate with your whole DevOps system and pipeline. These additional services won't be covered in this book, but I highly recommend you shop around to see which service satisfies the needs of your company.

One important point when considering your container registry is where you are going to run your containers. This single item might be the only thing you need to know to choose which container registry to use. If you decide to run your containers on Microsoft's cloud, Azure, you might want to use the Azure Container Registry simply because the integration will be easier and the proximity between the container host and the container registry results in faster startup times. If you are running your containers on-premises, there might be other aspects to consider, such as the additional services mentioned earlier. There might even be the case where you will end up with multiple container registries if you decide for a multi-cloud approach. For demonstration purposes of this book, we will be using Azure Container Registry. Keep in mind that while some aspects of the demos here are Azure specific, the concepts and especially the docker commands are valid for all OCI-compliant container registries.

After creating a container image you want to make available for all your container hosts, you will have to push the image to a container registry to then pull this image on subsequent container hosts. There are two types of container registries you might be using: public and private. Public container registries – also known as public repositories or repos – are container registries that anyone can pull images from. Private registries on the other hand will require that you authenticate before pulling images from that repo. However, for pushing images, you will always have to authenticate. Let's take a look at the pull process.

Earlier in this chapter, we introduced the Server Core container image. That image and its available tags can be found in the public Docker Hub repo from Microsoft: https://hub.docker.com/_/microsoft-windows-servercore. You will see that there are multiple tags available for this image – SAC, LTSC 2019, LTSC 2016, and so on.

If you'd like to have the image for Server Core LTSC 2019 available for use in your container host, you'd run the following command:

```
PS C:> docker pull mcr.microsoft.com/windows/servercore:ltsc2019
```

Docker pull is the command used to pull container images from a registry to your container host. The first thing I want you to notice is that I did not have to log into this registry. This is because this repo from Microsoft is open to whoever wants to pull its images. The next thing to notice is that the image name has its URL so Docker knows where to pull from regardless of where that registry resides – Azure, Docker Hub, AWS, and so on. Finally, different from the image you created on your container host, this image is stored using the name of its repo, so when you decide to use it, you'll have to use the whole name. We'll cover this when explaining pushing.

In the preceding example, if you want to pull from other registries or other images, all you have to do is to replace the image name and its tag. If you do not provide a tag, the "latest" tag will be pulled. Remember, however, that using the "latest" might lead to undesired situations, so whenever possible, specify a tag that you want.

If I want to pull from a private registry, I must log into that registry before pulling (or pushing for that matter). Here's how you do that:

```
PS C:> docker login mytestregistry.azurecr.io
```

The preceding command will start an authentication process between your session and the registry you want to use. Here is the output of the preceding command after username and password were provided:

```
Username (00000000-0000-0000-0000-000000000000): mytestregistry
Password:
WARNING! Your password will be stored unencrypted in C:\Users\[username]\.
docker\config.json.
Configure a credential helper to remove this warning. See
https://docs.docker.com/engine/reference/commandline/login/#credentials-store

Login Succeeded
```

Although the authentication was successful, it's important to follow the documentation described in the output of the preceding command. This is because docker will store the credentials you just entered in clear text in your container host. Since the utilization of this is different depending on the OS you are using and there are multiple forms of implementing it depending on your environment, this implementation is out of the scope of this book. In the case of Azure, a more secure option is to authenticate against the registry using your Azure credential and Azure PowerShell or the Azure CLI. We will discuss this in more detail in Chapter 6.

Once authenticated, you can push images to your registry. However, before pushing the image, you must match the name of the image with the registry you want to push it to. In our example, we have an image in our container host named mycontainerimage:v1, and our registry URL is mytestregistry.azurecr.io. Here is what we need to run:

```
PS C:> docker tag mycontainerimage:v1 mytestregistry.azurecr.io/
mycontainerimage:v1
```

The docker tag command will let you rename your container image and tag to whatever you describe. An interesting aspect of the docker tag command is that instead of renaming the image instance itself, you will now see two images, the original one and the recently tagged. Because docker uses the layering mechanism discussed previously, there's no additional footprint in the container host disk – the layers are still the same, but with two images in the container host.

By matching the container image name to the container registry, we can now push it using

```
PS C:> docker push mytestregistry.azurecr.io/mycontainerimage:v1
```

The preceding command should work if you have already logged to the registry previously. You can now go check your registry and confirm if the image is available for other container hosts to use. On a different container host, you can now run the following:

```
PS C:\> docker login mytestregistry.azurecr.io
Username (00000000-0000-0000-0000-000000000000): mytestregistry
Password:
WARNING! Your password will be stored unencrypted in C:\Users\[username]\.
docker\config.json.
```

Configure a credential helper to remove this warning. See
https://docs.docker.com/engine/reference/commandline/login/#credentials-store

Login Succeeded

PS C:\> docker pull mytestregistry.azurecr.io/mycontainerimage:v1

You can now use the image created on another container host in subsequent host.

Process isolation and hypervisor isolation

Shifting gears, so far we discussed many advantages of using containers including the isolation between each container and its host. Going back to Figure 1-2, it is clear that containers provide way less overhead when compared to VMs. However, VMs still have one upside: they offer complete isolation between not only each VM but also the host itself. For a multi-tenant environment (such as cloud environments), that's a must-have. If one of the VMs is compromised, the host is still protected and an attacker in theory can't get access to the parent partition – the virtualization host OS. With containers, that's not exactly true. In fact, in theory a compromised container can lead to an attack to the container host. Ironically, to solve that problem in the cloud, you end up building a container host as a VM. Still the workloads running on that container host VM are all yours, so to some extent, you trust the content and workload of each container. However, a cloud provider would never host workloads from different customers in the same container host VM, neither on physical hosts. For multi-tenancy workloads, a solution is needed, but before we go into the details, let's explore the process isolation mode, which both Linux and Windows implement.

We covered already how containers have their own view of the file system and registry. We also discussed that the kernel is shared. This is true for the mode known as process isolation. To demonstrate that, I started three containers on my container host. Here is the output of the docker ps command that lists all containers running on a host:

```
PS C:> docker ps
CONTAINER ID   IMAGE                    COMMAND                     CREATED
    STATUS            PORTS                   NAMES
c2653616bb33   mycontainerimage:v1    "C:\\ServiceMonitor.e..."   25 hours ago
    Up 25 hours       0.0.0.0:8091->80/tcp    testcontainer3
```

```
5a3c26421acc  mycontainerimage:v1  "C:\\ServiceMonitor.e…"    2 days ago
    Up 2 days         0.0.0.0:8082->80/tcp   testcontainer2
6388527c6744  mycontainerimage:v1  "C:\\ServiceMonitor.e..."  3 days ago
    Up 3 days         0.0.0.0:8083->80/tcp   testcontainer1
```

The preceding containers are all sharing the same container host kernel while isolated from each other. If we go inside the container and check for the file system, this is what we have:

```
PS C:\> dir

    Directory: C:\

Mode              LastWriteTime         Length Name
----              -------------         ------ ----
d-r---        4/12/2020    8:39 PM             Program Files
d-----        4/12/2020    8:38 PM             Program Files (x86)
d-r---        4/12/2020    8:40 PM             Users
d-----         5/1/2020   12:10 PM             Windows
-a----        9/15/2018    2:42 AM       5510 License.txt
```

This is completely different from what I have in my container host. For example, the folder we talked about earlier, C:\MyWebSite, is not listed there. These file system and folder structure are only visible inside the container. Another important thing is that this folder structure includes items that are important for the container to run. For example, let's look at the Users folder:

```
PS C:\> cd .\Users\
PS C:\Users> dir

    Directory: C:\Users

Mode              LastWriteTime         Length Name
----              -------------         ------ ----
d-----        4/24/2020    2:50 PM             Administrator
d-----         5/1/2020   12:10 PM             ContainerAdministrator
d-----        4/12/2020    8:40 PM             ContainerUser
d-r---        4/12/2020    8:39 PM             Public
```

Another example is when you check the registry inside the container:

```
PS C:\Users> $env:path
C:\Windows\system32;C:\Windows;C:\Windows\System32\Wbem;C:\Windows\
System32\WindowsPowerShell\v1.0\;C:\Windows\System32\OpenSSH\;C:\Users\
ContainerAdministrator\AppData\Local\Microsoft\WindowsApps
```

Let's compare that to our container host:

```
PS C:\ > $env:path
C:\windows\system32;C:\windows;C:\windows\System32\Wbem;C:\windows\
System32\WindowsPowerShell\v1.0\;C:\windows\System32\OpenSSH\;C:\Program
Files\Microsoft SQL Server\110\Tools\Binn\;C:\Program Files\Microsoft SQL
Server\120\Tools\Binn\;C:\Program Files\Docker;C:\Program Files\Git\cmd;C:\
Users\myusername\AppData\Local\Microsoft\WindowsApps;C:\Users\myusername\
AppData\Local\Programs\Microsoft VS Code\bin;C:\Users\myusername\AppData\
Local\GitHubDesktop\bin;C:\Program Files (x86)\GitHub CLI\
```

The results from checking the path inside the container and on the container host are different even though the container is sharing the same kernel. So the isolation we talked about for file system and registry is represented here. Now let's look at something else:

```
PS C:\> Get-Process | measure

Count      : 286
Average    :
Sum        :
Maximum    :
Minimum    :
Property   :
```

The preceding command is the return of get-process on the container host, which shows us how many processes are running. Let's look at the same inside the container:

```
PS C:\> Get-Process | measure

Count      : 21
Average    :
Sum        :
```

```
Maximum  :
Minimum  :
Property :
```

That is an astonishing low number of process for a Windows image. Inside the container, we only have 21 processes running. However, more importantly is checking what the host can see from the containers. Let's look in more detail at one core component on Windows:

```
PS C:\> Get-Process -Name smss
```

```
Handles    NPM(K)    PM(K)     WS(K)     CPU(s)    Id     SI    ProcessName
-------    ------    -----     -----     ------    --     --    -----------
50         3         476       1184      0.14      5084   0     smss
```

SMSS stands for Microsoft Session Manager Subsystem and is a core component in the Windows OS. This process manages the startup of all user sessions in Windows, and there should be only one in each deployment of Windows. The preceding result is from the command launched from inside the container. Nothing new here, but let's take a look at the same thing from the container host:

```
PS C:\> Get-Process -Name smss
```

```
Handles    NPM(K)    PM(K)     WS(K)     CPU(s)    Id     SI    ProcessName
-------    ------    -----     -----     ------    --     --    -----------
56         3         560       1284      0.33      388    0     smss
50         3         472       1184      0.11      3320   0     smss
50         3         468       1184      0.14      3976   0     smss
50         3         476       1184      0.14      5084   0     smss
```

Here's a question: If every Windows OS has only one smss process running, how come this container host has four of it? The answer is because the container host can see the process inside the containers using process isolation. In fact, you can see that although these are the same processes, they have different process IDs. In fact, the one we checked inside the container has process ID 5084, and we see the same process on the container host. Keep in mind that the container host can see not only the smss processes but all processes running inside the containers.

These examples are all to demonstrate that although process isolation provides a level of isolation between containers and container hosts, it still provides some level of commonality that could, in theory, be exploited by an attacker. Prevention against those attacks is pretty much like securing a regular deployment of Windows: keep your machine updated with security updates and have an anti-malware in place and updated, as well as security baselines in place for the workloads you are running. However, if you really want to ensure total isolation between container and container host, Microsoft provides another level of isolation: hypervisor isolation.

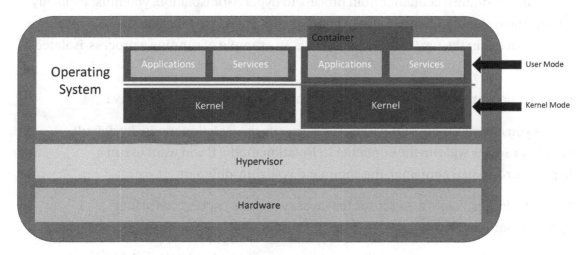

Figure 1-5. *Hypervisor-isolated containers*

Take a moment to compare Figure 1-5 to Figure 1-2. You will notice the main difference from each architecture is the fact that in process isolation the kernel used by the containers is shared – the container host kernel. On hypervisor-isolated containers, the container is wrapped on a purpose-built VM that has its own kernel. It's important to note that this purpose-built VM is not a regular Hyper-V VM. In fact, Microsoft even changed the nomenclature to avoid confusion.

When containers were first launched in Windows Server 2016, the nomenclature for the isolation modes were "Windows Containers" for process isolation and "Hyper-V containers" for hypervisor-isolated containers. This caused confusion in the market as many customers thought Hyper-V containers were VMs running containers – they are not. In fact, you will find that in some cases this purpose-built VM is also referenced as utility VM or UVM.

This UVM is not something you can manage directly as a regular Hyper-V VM. In fact, if you open Hyper-V Manager, you won't see that VM in there. There are ways to interact with the UVM for managing purposes, and we will explore that in a future chapter. For now, the important thing to keep in mind is that you can manage containers running on these UVMs the same way you manage process-isolated containers. There is no difference between the containers themselves; the only difference is when you decide to deploy the container. The whole process of creating a container image explained in the previous section is exactly the same.

To differentiate a container from process to hypervisor isolation, you must explicitly specify the isolation mode when starting your container. We will explore more the docker run command in the next chapter, but here is an example of running a process-isolated container:

```
PS C:\> docker run -d --name mytestcontainer mycontainerimage:v1
```

As you can see, there's no parameter to specify the isolation mode. By default, Windows Server will run the container in isolation mode. If you want to run a hypervisor-isolated container, the command is slightly different:

```
PS C:\> docker run -d --isolation=hyperv --name mytestcontainer
mycontainerimage:v1
```

The --isolation parameter will start the container inside a UVM and run the container specified in the docker run command. As you can see, we're starting from the same container image.

Keep in mind that hypervisor isolation provides a higher level of isolation, but that comes with a price. Because of the way process-isolated containers share a common kernel, they have a lower requirement in terms of resources when you spin up multiple containers. That is not true for hypervisor isolation. Also, every time a hypervisor-isolated container starts, the UVM has to start as well, which adds a few seconds. While this doesn't compare to a regular VM, it does take more time and resources than a process-isolated container.

Process-isolated containers are the default mode for Windows Server, but Windows 10 has the opposite behavior. In fact, at first Windows 10 only had the hypervisor isolation mode, and in Windows 10 October 2018 Update, Microsoft introduced the option to run process-isolated containers. Still, you need to directly specify the --isolation=process flag in order to run on that mode. We will explore more on why this happens in the next chapter where we will cover matching container image and host versions.

Licensing of Windows Containers

Now that you have a good understanding on what Windows Containers are, how they differentiate from VMs, and some scenarios on which you'd benefit from using containers, it is important to understand the licensing implications of using Windows Containers. Luckily, licensing Windows containers is not much different than licensing Windows Server VMs.

As you know, Windows Server has two main editions: Windows Server Standard and Windows Server Datacenter. There are other editions, such as Windows Server Essentials, but they don't necessarily apply in the containers space. Before we move on, please note that I did not mention version in the preceding text, such as 2016 or 2019. The licensing model is the same for both; the difference in licensing Windows containers will be in the edition, which is apart from the version.

If you ever looked into licensing Windows Server, you probably know that there's a distinction between what a license is and the software itself. The license of Windows Server is a piece of paper that grants you the rights of running an instance of Windows Server – also referred to as Operating System Environment (OSE). An OSE is a deployment of Windows Server regardless if it is virtualized or not.

What that means is that a piece of paper might allow you to run multiple instances of Windows Server. For example, with one single license of Windows Server, you might be able to deploy an instance of it on the physical host and inside one or more VMs. You will not be able to deploy multiple instances of Windows Server on different physical machines with one single license. The same way, you might need more than one single license associated to a physical host to properly license it.

In 2015, Microsoft changed the way you count how many licenses of Windows Server you need per physical machine from processors to cores on that specific host. In the past, a Windows Server license was necessary for every two processors, regardless of the number of cores. If your server has two processors, you were required to have one license of Windows Server, which covers those two processors. A server with six processors would require three licenses of Windows Server. See that we are talking about a piece of paper here. The installation key itself is the same for the host and VMs on that machine. The main difference from Standard to Datacenter then was the number of Windows Server OSEs allowed by each edition. Standard allows you to run up to two Windows Server VMs per host, plus the host OS itself. Datacenter allows unlimited Windows Server VMs, plus the host OS itself.

However, today you must license not only the processors but the cores of your server as well. Today, a Windows Server license covers two processors with 8 cores per processor, with a total of 16 cores. If your server has more than eight cores per processor, you can buy separate two-core packs. These two-core packs are one-eight of the price of a regular Windows Server license. However, the number of VMs allowed by each edition, Standard and Datacenter, is still the same. Standard allows you to run up to two Windows Server VMs per license associated with a host, and Datacenter allows you to run unlimited Windows Server VMs.

Unfortunately, there are multiple variables in the pricing of Windows Server that will affect the final price of each license. Different customers can get different prices based on volume purchase, established contract, discount level, and so on. For that reason, it is not in the scope of this book to make a recommendation on which edition to buy. You should check Microsoft's licensing page (`www.microsoft.com/en-us/cloud-platform/windows-server-pricing`) and contact your Microsoft or partner representative to make a decision.

The question is, how does this all affect your container deployment? The answer to this question is that process-isolated containers are unlimited under the Standard and Datacenter edition, but hypervisor-isolated containers are treated as VMs, which means you can run up to two hypervisor containers per Windows Server Standard license and unlimited hypervisor-isolated containers with the Windows Server Datacenter license.

At the end of the day, the number of licenses required per host will be a combination of how many VMs, containers, processors, and cores you have per host. Let's look at an example.

You have a container host with four processors, eight cores per processor, and you plan to run 50 hypervisor-isolated containers. In this case, you need two Windows Server licenses, but the question is: Which edition? Standard or Datacenter?

Since you are planning to run 50 hypervisor-isolated containers per host, you are probably going to go with the Datacenter edition. The main reason for that is because you will need 25 licenses of Windows Server Standard, regardless of the processor/core count. If for the same scenario you were planning to run only four hypervisor-isolated containers or only process-isolated containers, then you should probably check the Standard edition as the cost would probably be lower.

Another important component to keep in mind when licensing your environment is something you can add to your licensing contract: Software Assurance (SA). SA is an add-on to Microsoft licenses that provide many benefits. Historically, the main benefit companies get from SA is the ability to upgrade to the next version of Windows Server (or the software in question, since SA is not exclusive to Windows Server). What that means is when you buy a Windows Server license under a contract, you can add the SA benefit. The SA benefit will cast you 25% of the total of the Windows Server license for a three-year contract. Since Microsoft launches a new version of Windows Server every 2–3 years, you end up paying less in the long run.

For containers, the SA benefit has another upside. Today, Microsoft releases Windows Server in two channels: Semi-Annual Channel (SAC) and Long-Term Servicing Channel (LTSC). The main difference for each is in the scenarios covered, the release cadence, and support policy.

If you've been using Windows Server for years, you are used to Windows Server being launched every 2–3 years – Windows Servers 2008, 2008 R2, 2012, 2012 R2, 2016, and so on. All these releases are part of the LTSC channel. In addition to this cadence, these releases have all the Windows Server roles and features and have 5 years of mainstream support and 5 more years of extended support. In 2017, Microsoft introduced the SAC for Windows Server. This channel provides two releases per year, is focused on containers and application development scenarios, and has 18 months of support. Yes, you read that correctly: there is a new version of Windows Server twice per year. At this point, I see many Windows admins skeptical about upgrading in such fast pace. However, keep in mind that you don't have to update your server twice a year. You have to update before the 18-month support expires. This is way shorter than the regular 10-year support policy for LTSC, but on the other hand, it does allow you to get new innovation faster. Believe, in the container world, this will be a must. There is way too much development happening out there in the container, Kubernetes, and microservices space, so the SAC is a response to that fast pace.

However, oftentimes I see customers not having to deal with all this by simply running their Windows Server container hosts on cloud environments, such as Microsoft Azure. In Azure, you don't have to deal with the licensing of Windows Server, neither Standard nor Datacenter comparisons, simply because Azure charges you on a per-minute basis, based on the size (cores, memory, disk, network) of your VM.

In addition to that, if you already bought a Windows Server license to use on-premises and have SA associated to that Windows Server license, you get an additional benefit called Azure Hybrid Benefit (AHB). AHB allows you to get an additional discount on the cost of Windows Server VMs on Azure because you already have a Windows

Server license. You can find more information on this here: `https://azure.microsoft.com/en-us/pricing/hybrid-benefit/`.

Hopefully at this point, you are equipped to make a better decision on how to approach the use of Windows Containers in your environment. Now it is time to pull up the sleeves and dive deep into the usage of Windows containers – which is what we will do in the next chapter.

## CHAPTER 2

Getting started with Windows Containers and Docker

If you are like me and you went through the whole Chapter 1, then you must be eager to see all the concepts you learned in action. Not to worry – in this chapter, we will start the journey of diving deep into the Windows containers world. At this point, you know that the way we interact with containers is through a Command Prompt or PowerShell command line based on the Docker commands. We covered what Docker is in the previous chapter and you already saw some interaction with containers, but before we start using it, there are just some final things I wanted to go over.

As explained earlier, Docker is a company that provides a toolset for managing containers. However, Docker is more than that. In fact, in November 2019, Docker went through a major reorganization on which part of its business was sold. What was called Docker Enterprise Services went to a company called Mirantis, and Docker is now focused on the developer experience. For the purposes of this book, this is relevant so you understand that there might be cases on which we will be covering items that might not be part of Docker, Inc. anymore.

More importantly though, it is important to understand the architecture of the components you will be installing when running containers on your hosts and what are their roles not just for trying out containers but moving forward when you take the next step and decide to run your containers with an orchestrator.

V. Ramos Apolinario, *Windows Containers for IT Pros*, https://doi.org/10.1007/978-1-4842-6686-1_2

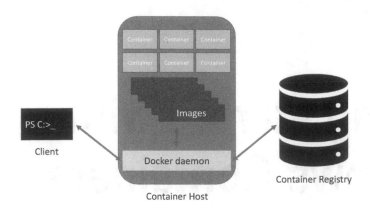

Figure 2-1. Docker daemon

As you can see in Figure 2-1, the Docker daemon is an important entity as it is responsible to listen to the commands from the clients, deal with images and containers on the host, as well as pull and push images from registries.

However, the Docker daemon as an entity has its own layers built in. As part of the daemon, we have an API on which other applications, such as orchestrators, can call into. We also have a container runtime standard, which in the case of Docker is called "dockerd." Finally, we have another standard on which the docker daemon plays an important role, which is to support plugins for storage and networking. We will explore this last piece in further chapters.

The main reason why we are covering this is because in this book you will learn the essentials of Windows containers and how they work as the instance on which your application runs. When you deploy an application on a production environment, there are other items you might need to consider, such as high availability, load balance, node management, and so much more. For VMs, usually you get all that from the platform you are running. For example, if you are running Hyper-V, you have Failover Cluster, System Center, Windows Admin Center, and many other components from Microsoft to build your infrastructure. The same goes for VMware with ESXi, vCenter, vSphere, vSAN, and so on. With containers, however, that's not exactly like that.

In the early days of containers, Docker established not only the container runtime (dockerd as part of the docker daemon) and container packaging (docker file) standards, but it also introduced another component called Swarm. Swarm is docker's orchestrator tool, which takes care of the items we just talked about, like failover, load balance, node management, and so on. Along with Docker Swarm, other orchestrators came up, more famously Kubernetes and Service Fabric. If you heard about Kubernetes, then you can probably realize that it became the "de facto" orchestrator for containerized applications. Kubernetes (also known as K8s), however, does not provide a container runtime. Instead, it calls into that layer. As of the writing of this book, there is an open question in the orchestrator world on which container runtime will be the next "de facto" standard to rise. So far, everything points to containerd, which is an open source container runtime.

The interesting thing about the container runtime is that you don't necessarily interact directly with it. If you decide to use K8s as your orchestrator and containerd as the runtime, you will perform all actions via K8s, totally abstracting the interaction with the runtime. The same thing goes if you decide to continue to use the dockerd runtime. Furthermore, the container image you build is also the same. For example, you build your container image using docker build to read the docker file. You then push this image to a registry. From that point on, it doesn't matter what is the orchestrator and the container runtime you decide to use. They all will run the same container image standard you created – at least for the foreseeable future. It might be the case that one day the container and container orchestration community decide to change this. But this is only speculation; we'll have to wait and see.

Deploying your first container host

If you are a developer – which at this point of the book, I hope you are not – then for you the journey with containers starts with the application itself and how you prepare it to be built as a container. However, if you are an IT Pro, your journey starts with the container host on which your container images will reside, and your containers will run.

There are two scenarios in which you will run containers in the Windows universe: A Windows 10 machine can be used to run containers for testing and development purposes. Or a Windows Server host can be used for testing purposes, but also for production environments. We will cover the two options in this section, so you know how to deploy it correctly in both situations.

Docker on Windows 10

On a Windows 10 environment, you will be using a version of Docker called Docker Desktop for Windows, which is a free tool provided by Docker. To download the tool, you can access `https://hub.docker.com/editions/community/docker-ce-desktop-windows`.

Docker Desktop, as mentioned earlier, is focused on development environments and provides additional tools, such as integration with Swarm, the ability to run Linux containers, and other functionalities. To install it, open the file executable downloaded from the preceding link. The first screen you will is this.

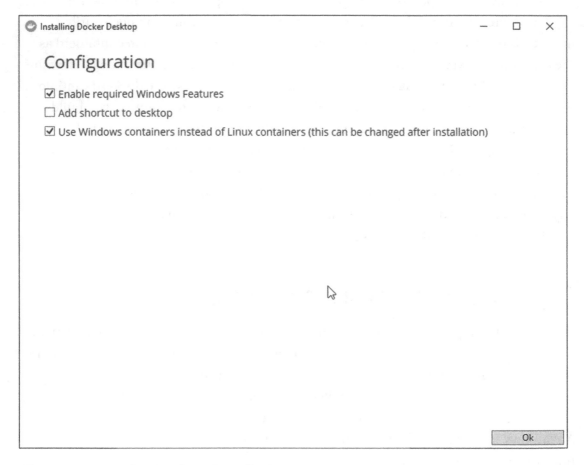

Figure 2-2. *Docker Desktop installation*

In Figure 2-2, make sure you keep the option "Enable required Windows Features" selected as this will install the Containers feature on Windows. Also, Docker Desktop is able to run both Windows and Linux containers on your Windows 10 host, but not at the same time, so keep the option "Use Windows containers instead of Linux containers" selected.

After clicking Ok, Docker will go through the installation process and will ask to close and restart your machine.

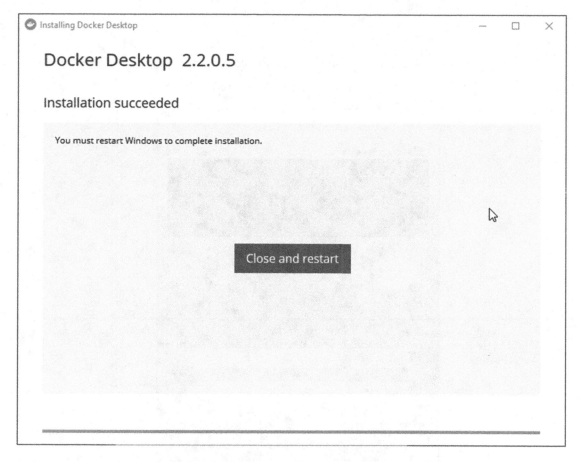

Figure 2-3. *Close and restart Docker Desktop installation, as shown in Figure 2-3.*

After you restart your Windows 10 machine and log back in, Docker Desktop will start, and you will see the Docker icon on the system tray. Also, you will see the Welcome page on your desktop, as shown in Figure 2-4.

Figure 2-4. *Docker Desktop Welcome page*

Docker Desktop allows you to log with your Docker ID credential, which makes it easier when you want to push your container images to the Docker Hub. Also, by right-clicking the Docker Desktop icon in the system tray, you get easy access to some interesting functionalities, such as changing the default from Windows to Linux containers, opening the Dashboard to show you the running containers, checking for updates, and many other settings. These settings are all configurable via CLI, and we will explore some of it in the upcoming chapters.

Docker on Windows Server

The main difference between installing Docker on a Windows 10 and Windows Server machine is that for Windows 10 you have a nice Desktop feature with system tray icon and some pretty UI to use. For Windows Server, the expectation is that you install Docker, deploy your containers, and manage everything either remotely or through the orchestrator policies and configuration. Just like any other workload on a server, the best practice is to deploy the minimal configuration needed and perform any interaction and management remotely.

In the last chapter, we discussed SAC vs. LTSC releases of Windows Server. The SAC release of Windows Server was created to meet the need for containers to get updates more frequently. It has a new release every six months, and each release is supported for 18 months. One other aspect of the SAC release is that it only comes in the Server Core installation option – there's no GUI for you to play with. However, remember two things: First, you don't want to deploy more than you need for running containers. Second, the interaction with containers will be via CLI anyway, so going with Server Core is probably your best bet for production environments. For testing, it's fine to stick with Server with Desktop experience and its GUI, but for that case, you'll have to stick with a new release (LTSC) every 2–3 years.

The installation itself of Docker and the Containers feature on Windows Server is also a bit different than on Windows 10. There are two steps for the installation, and they should be performed on an elevated PowerShell session:

```
Install-Module -Name DockerMsftProvider -Repository PSGallery -Force
```

The preceding command will download the Docker module from the PowerShell gallery. Different from regular features on Windows, Docker is not a native module on Windows and Windows Server, hence the need to keep it outside of the installation.

Many times, I see questions from people who enabled the Containers feature on Windows Server, and they don't know what to do next. That's why instead of just enabling the feature, you also need to deploy Docker. The following command will do both:

```
Install-Package -Name docker -ProviderName DockerMsftProvider
```

This will take a few moments, and when completed, you need to restart your server. You can do that via the regular UI on a Server with Desktop experience or via PowerShell:

```
Restart-Computer -Force
```

Once your server restarts, you can start playing with Windows containers.

Getting started with Docker

You now have a fully functional container host to play with Windows containers. From now on, we will perform all actions on a Windows Server host, but keep in mind that all the commands should work on a Windows 10 machine as well. The only difference, as covered in the previous chapter, will be that on a Windows 10 machine the default isolation mode will be hypervisor, so you need to explicitly inform if you want process isolation.

The first thing you probably want to do at this point is to just get a container running, right? Let's take a look at how to do that. On an elevated PowerShell session, run the following command:

```
PS C:\> docker run -d --name myfirstcontainer mcr.microsoft.com/windows/
servercore:ltsc2019
```

If you simply installed the container host and ran the preceding command, you are probably not overly impressed by the time it took to get the container running – in fact, probably the opposite. As you have probably noticed during the execution, Docker had to pull the necessary layers of the container image you started your container from. This is because the container host comes without any container images pre-populated. Since the Server Core image has a few gigs in size, it's understandable that it took a while to run the container. Here is the output of the command on a brand-new container host:

```
Unable to find image 'mcr.microsoft.com/windows/servercore:ltsc2019'
locally
ltsc2019: Pulling from windows/servercore
65014b3c3121: Pull complete
eac6fba788c9: Pull complete
Digest: sha256:2ecf1e2987b91b41f576afd7f56aa40c9ddbc691d7b6b066c64d8f27
fb3070ca
```

```
Status: Downloaded newer image for mcr.microsoft.com/windows/
servercore:ltsc2019
5504603f938be09a6c04f936fb9561e1780e08b4d37407ee413f962e9ec1bf58
```

As you can get from the output, Docker did not find the image locally, so it had to download all the layers for that container image. The next time you run the command to start a new container from that image, it will be way faster. Now let's take a look at the command itself.

All commands for using Docker either on Windows 10 or Windows Server will start with "docker" itself. In the case of spinning up a new container, we use the parameter "run," which not only creates the new container but also starts the container. In the preceding command, we used the "-d" parameter to inform docker that this container will run "detached," which means docker should keep this container running. However, while the run command will execute the container, if the container is expected to execute something and doesn't have an outstanding service or program to continue to run, then the container is expected to simply enter a stopped state. With containers, there are many situations on which you spin up a container, the application inside the container runs, and the container stops after that.

After the "-d" parameter, we specified "--name." This parameter is not required, but it helps in finding your container later. If you don't provide a name to your container, docker will do that. (Funny fact: Docker has a library of funny names, and it allocates it to your containers if you don't specify one.)

Next, we provided the image we wanted to use as a template to create this container. Here, there is an interesting thing: although we're using a PowerShell session, docker does not follow the PowerShell notation, so as long as you put the necessary information in the right place, docker will capture the configuration to run the command. That's why we simply pass the value for the container image parameter without calling the parameter itself. If you remember from the previous chapter, all containers are created based on a container image. In this case, we used the LTSC 2019 image of the Server Core base container image.

This image we just used has an interesting configuration. The docker file used to create this image does not specify what process or service is supposed to run inside the container. For that reason, the container is exited right after it's started. Here is another curious difference between containers and VMs: a VM runs the OS regardless if there's an application, service, or process listening to a client/remote calls. For containers, if there's no entry point, the container will be stopped. The entry point can be specified either in the run or start commands or inside the docker file so you don't have to call the process or service.

The "docker ps" command shows you the running containers. However, if you run this command for the container you just created, you will notice that it doesn't return anything. Instead, you will have to append the "-a" parameter, which shows you all containers, regardless of its state. Here's the output for the command:

```
PS C:\> docker ps -a | fl
CONTAINER ID   IMAGE
COMMAND                        CREATED        STATUS     PORTS           NAMES
8277cc187453   mcr.microsoft.com/windows/servercore:ltsc2019
"c:\\windows\\system32..."   5 minutes ago  Exited (0) 5 minutes ago
myfirstcontainer
```

Notice the status for this container is showing "Exited (0) 5 minutes ago". The command tab represents the service or process for the container to run, and in this case, it was the Command Prompt at C:\windows\system32\cmd.exe. Part of the path is omitted at the preceding output, but that's the default for the preceding configuration.

Now let's see another example. Let's run the following command:

```
PS C:\> docker pull mcr.microsoft.com/windows/servercore/
iis:windowsservercore-ltsc2019
```

The preceding command will pull the IIS image for a Server Core on Windows Server 2019 LTSC. Look at the output – there's an interesting thing here:

```
windowsservercore-ltsc2019: Pulling from windows/servercore/iis
65014b3c3121: Already exists
eac6fba788c9: Already exists
71ac5891d8f6: Pull complete
5ff6f3d1fce7: Pull complete
1778fe22ba9e: Pull complete
Digest: sha256:3cfed0e8c332365ede95b0040a80a8b4155472b7d8a8c4e191fd5203db
9f3523
Status: Downloaded newer image for mcr.microsoft.com/windows/servercore/
iis:windowsservercore-ltsc2019
mcr.microsoft.com/windows/servercore/iis:windowsservercore-ltsc2019
```

Noticed the first two layers docker was pulling? Noticed the "Already exists"? Can you guess why that is? Yes, these are the same layers as the previous Server Core image based on Windows Server 2019 LTSC. What that means is that the IIS image has only three additional layers on top of the previous layers of the Server Core image. The pull process should have been way faster now since there are not many changes. If you are really interested in understanding how the IIS image was created, you can even see the docker file Microsoft used to create it. It is available at `https://github.com/Microsoft/iis-docker/blob/master/windowsservercore-ltsc2019/Dockerfile`, and here is its output from that URL:

```
# escape=`
FROM mcr.microsoft.com/windows/servercore:ltsc2019

RUN powershell -Command `
    Add-WindowsFeature Web-Server; `
    Invoke-WebRequest -UseBasicParsing -Uri "https://dotnetbinaries.blob.
    core.windows.net/servicemonitor/2.0.1.10/ServiceMonitor.exe" -OutFile
    "C:\ServiceMonitor.exe"

EXPOSE 80

ENTRYPOINT ["C:\\ServiceMonitor.exe", "w3svc"]
```

We will explore docker files and possible constructs for it in more detail later in this chapter and throughout the book. For now, look at two things: First, there are three commands after the FROM line. Those three commands are represented in the three layers we pulled earlier. Also, the last line has "ENTRYPOINT". Notice the construct of this docker file specifies both ServiceMonitor.exe and w3svc. ServiceMonitor.exe is a Windows executable provided by Microsoft specifically for container environments. Its role is to monitor the w3svc service and its state. The w3svc service is the IIS service itself. What we can conclude from this is that if you simply spin up a container based on the IIS image, you will get a container that will not stop after you create it. Let's see this in action:

```
PS C:\> docker run -d -p 8080:80 --name myiiscontainer mcr.microsoft.com/
windows/servercore/iis:windowsservercore-ltsc2019
c979708db860735ed04705ebd636ce8373cbbc72353b290dfa90ddfa4fb5bd77
PS C:\> docker ps
```

```
CONTAINER ID          IMAGE
COMMAND                     CREATED          STATUS              PORTS
NAMES
c979708db860          mcr.microsoft.com/windows/servercore/
iis:windowsservercore-ltsc2019    "C:\\ServiceMonitor.e…"    6 seconds ago
Up 4 seconds          0.0.0.0:8080->80/tcp    myiiscontainer
```

Now we can see the container running with the "docker ps" command. However, you must have noticed a different parameter in the docker run command. The "-p" parameter specifies which ports you want to open for this container. By default, the network for containers is a Network Address Translation (NAT) network type. NAT is a translation implementation on which you have a public IP address exposed to the network of the host and a private IP address for one or multiple instances behind this IP. You are probably familiar with this as this is how routers/firewalls work for connecting multiple LAN-connected devices to WAN/Internet on IPv4. For containers, what this means is that the containers will receive a private IP that is not routable to the public network, like the IP address from the host. With that, to access a port that has a service exposed in the container, we translate the IP and port of the host to the IP and port of the container. This must be a 1-to-1 mapping. In our preceding example, we are mapping the port 8080 of the container host to the port 80 of the container, which is the HTTP port on which IIS is listening. Note: The docker file from which the IIS image was created already specified a port 80, so we did not have to necessarily specify this here. However, if we did not specify a port, docker would use a random port for that. We will go into more detail on how networking is configured and other options in Chapter 4.

The result of everything in the preceding text is that you now have a container running an instance of IIS listening at the port 8080 on the container host. If you open a browser and target the container host IP address on port 8080, this is what you'll see.

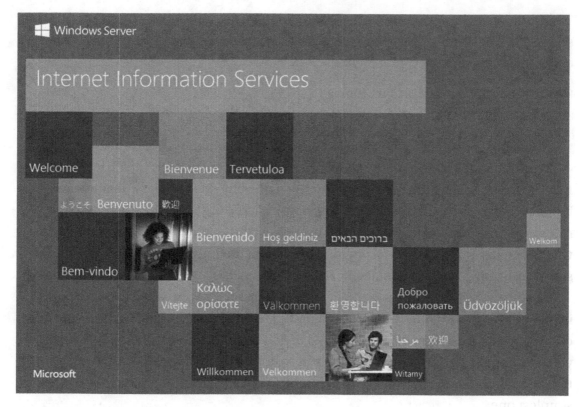

Figure 2-5. *IIS default welcome page*

The preceding page in Figure 2-5 is the default IIS welcome page and is shown when you don't have another website or web application configured.

If you want to stop a running container, you can use the following command:

```
PS C:\> docker stop myiiscontainer
myiiscontainer
```

In the preceding example, we used the name of the container to tell docker which container to stop. If you did not specify a name to the container when you created it, you can either use the name docker provided to it or its container ID. Both can be obtained from the docker ps command. After running the preceding command, the container entered a stopped state. To remove the container, you can run

```
PS C:\> docker rm myiiscontainer
myiiscontainer
```

If you try to remove the container before stopping it, you'll get an error message saying you can't remove the container while it's in a running state. To avoid that, you can either manually stop the container or use

```
PS C:\> docker rm myiiscontainer -f
myiiscontainer
```

The "-f" parameter will force the removal of the container regardless of its state.

Up until now, we instantiated containers, but we did not directly interact with it. In fact, there won't be many times on which you might need to open a container and interact with it. As we discussed in the previous chapter, containers are supposed to run based on a container image that has everything the container needs to run, execute whatever it has to do, and be decommissioned when it's time. If the application or service is needed, another container can be instantiated.

In some cases, however, you might need to interact directly with a container instance. This is particularly helpful when you are building a container image and one of the steps in the docker file fails. Instead of debugging the logs from the container, you can actually perform them manually in a running container and see the output of the command. There are many ways to interact with a running container. Here's the simplest one:

```
PS C:\> docker run --entrypoint powershell -it --name mycontainer mcr.
microsoft.com/windows/servercore:ltsc2019
```

The preceding command is very similar to the docker run commands we executed so far. The main difference is that we are adding two parameters: the "--entrypoint" and the "-it". The "-it" parameter indicates that you want an interactive session with this container. Along with that, when you add the "--entrypoint" parameter and specify PowerShell, you immediately enter a PowerShell session inside this container. You'll notice the PowerShell window will refresh and the context will change from wherever you were located at that moment to C:\ inside the container. If you type "dir", you will see the list of directories and files inside that container, not the host. To go back to the container host, type "exit".

One important aspect of working interactively with Windows containers is understanding what the entry point and what session you want to enter. Remember the Server Core image we're using doesn't have an entry point? So in this case, you don't even have to specify the parameter at the docker run command. You could use

```
PS C:\> docker run -it --name testcontainer mcr.microsoft.com/windows/
servercore:ltsc2019 powershell
```

This command would work exactly like the previous one. However, if you change the image you're using to an image that has an entry point specified in the docker file (such as the IIS image), the preceding command would fail. To avoid that, always use --entrypoint when interactively running a Windows container.

Another less common situation is when you have to open an interactive session with a container that has already been created and is already running. Let's say you created a container called testcontainer specifying the "-d" option and now you want to open an interactive session with it. For that, you can use the following:

```
PS C:\> docker exec --interactive testcontainer powershell
```

The preceding command will open the same PowerShell interactive session as before, but now with a container that was already created. Yet another variant is when you need to open an interactive session to a container is stopped. For that, you can use

```
PS C:\> docker start --interactive testcontainer
```

The docker start command will start the container, but the --interactive option will do the trick. Notice that in this case I didn't even have to specify the entry point. Here is a case that is a bit confusing: When I created this container, I specified the entry point as being PowerShell, so now I can go ahead and simply use the preceding command. However, if I did not specify that either in the docker file or in the run command, the docker start won't work as it does not support the --entrypoint parameter. The solution here is to use the docker exec command.

Using the option to run a container interactively will serve you a lot when you start to play with docker files – as we will discuss in our next section.

Understanding the docker file

We explored the concept of docker files in the previous chapter. Now let's look into a more useful example of how to use it. As explained previously, the docker file is pretty much a recipe describing how to prepare a container image so it can serve as a template for new containers.

Think the docker file as a script with instructions and arguments for those instructions. These instructions can be native commands, such as the ones covered in the previous chapter: FROM and WORKDIR. Or they can be a set of commands called by the RUN instructions. The RUN instruction is very useful and flexible, since you can call pretty much everything you want from it, such as PowerShell Command Prompt commands.

As explained, the docker file will be read by the docker build command from top to bottom – line by line. Each new line will represent a new layer so one of your goals with the docker file will be to execute the minimum amount of commands and lines as possible. That will ensure a smaller footprint for your container image. Don't worry if you don't get that at first. Right now, your target is to get a functional container image – you'll get the best practices with time.

As the first example in this book, we will use the simplest example we can probably find: a simple HTML file. For the purpose of this example, this file represents the entire application you want to containerize. In further examples, we will look into way more complex examples of course.

To get started, let's create a new folder to host our "application." From an elevated PowerShell session, type

```
PS C:\> New-Item -ItemType Directory -Path C:\MyApp
```

Now that you have a new folder for your application, let's create a new HTML file:

```
PS C:\> New-Item -ItemType File -Path C:\MyApp\MyApp.HTML
```

The preceding command created the file, but there's nothing in it. Using Notepad, open the file and type in some content so you can see it on the web browser later, such as

```
Hello World from Windows Containers! My App version1.0.
```

Save the file and close Notepad. See that a proper HTML file would have proper HTML notation, but for the purpose of this example, we'll keep the file as is.

Now, let's create a new dockerfile and store it at the same folder:

```
PS C:\> New-Item -ItemType File -Path C:\MyApp\dockerfile
```

Using Notepad again, open the file so we can add the instructions to it.

As explained in the previous chapter, all docker files will start with FROM. The question here is which base container image you want to use. Since this is a website, what we need is an image that has Windows, of course, but also IIS installed. In fact, you could use the Server Core one and install IIS to it, but that doesn't make a lot of sense since Microsoft already provides an IIS image. With that, our first line will be

```
FROM mcr.microsoft.com/windows/servercore/iis:windowsservercore-ltsc2019
```

Remember that all images are stored in the Docker Hub, so if you are not sure which image to use, you can quickly browse the Docker Hub and find it.

Now we need to copy the folder of our application to the container image. There are several ways of doing that:

- You could use RUN to have a PowerShell command create a new folder and then use COPY to copy the folder from the container host to the container image. In the COPY command, you'd have to specify the path for the destination, since there's nothing defined there.

- You could use WORKDIR to create the new folder in the container image and then COPY to copy the folder from the container host to the container image. This way, you don't have to specify the path since the context is already the working directory.

- You could use either RUN or WORKDIR to create the new folder and then use COPY to copy the folder from a network share.

- You could use a staging image, run a few commands, and then copy from this staging image to the final one only the necessary items. This is a more advanced option, and we will cover this and other best practices in Chapter 3.

With time, you will learn that each option provides different pros and cons. For this example, we will use the WORKDIR option:

```
WORKDIR C:\\inetPub\\wwwroot
```

Here, we need to pause for a moment to better understand what's going on. In the previous chapter, I talked about context and how on Linux systems this is more natural than Windows. For the specific case of Windows and Docker, the initial context will always be the C:\ drive, unless something else (such as the WORKDIR) is specified. However, you might have noticed that I used – in the example in the previous chapter –

the forward slash "/" character, rather than the back slash "\" traditionally used on Windows. This is because of the way Docker reads the file. When using context to omit the whole path, you should use forward slash, or "/". You would think that for full paths you'd use the traditional back slash "\" then, right? Well, not exactly. Yes, you should use back slash "\", but because of the way Docker reads the information, you need to use two each time. That way, if you decide to use the whole path, you should use something like "C:\\MyApp". In the preceding case, we are telling Docker that the working directory to use from there is C:\Inetpub\wwwroot, but we had to use two back slashes each time. There is a way to avoid that by specifying how Docker should read escapes in the docker file. We will also cover that in Chapter 3 along with other best practices.

Now, we have a base image that has IIS and has the folder on which to copy information to. So let's see how to copy that:

```
COPY . .
```

I know. As a Windows administrator myself, it's really weird to see the two dots in this command. But it really simplifies the process. All we're doing here is to tell Docker to copy the content from the folder on which the context is set. The first dot represents the context of the container host, and the second represents the context from the container image. If we were to see the paths here, they would be C:\MyApp* to C:\inetpub\wwwroot. It's easier to just use dots, right?

A traditional application would probably require more inputs, but our very simple HTML file doesn't. You can save the docker file and close Notepad. Now let's see our super application in action!

Deploying your first container

If you followed the instructions from the previous section, you should have everything in place to build your new image and new container. To start that process in the same elevated PowerShell session, let's navigate to the folder of the application to ensure everything is there:

```
PS C:\> cd C:\MyApp\
PS C:\MyApp> dir

    Directory: C:\MyApp
```

```
Mode                LastWriteTime         Length Name
----                -------------         ------ ----
-a----      5/22/2020    1:59 PM             114 dockerfile
-a----      5/22/2020    1:25 PM              55 MyApp.HTML
```

Notice we have the two files created in the previous section, so we're ready to build an image. We'll be using docker build for that:

```
PS C:\MyApp> docker build -t myappimage:v1 .
Sending build context to Docker daemon  3.072kB
Step 1/3 : FROM mcr.microsoft.com/windows/servercore/iis:windowsservercore-
ltsc2019
 ---> 1dfea62c25d8
Step 2/3 : WORKDIR C:\\InetPub\\WWWRoot
 ---> Running in 98a5fec2decf
Removing intermediate container 98a5fec2decf
 ---> eac04660bd88
Step 3/3 : COPY . .
 ---> 78fd07b50870
Successfully built 78fd07b50870
Successfully tagged myappimage:v1
```

The command we used here is the same we used in other examples already. We're using docker build, followed by the tag we're specifying for this image, and then indicating the context. The result is that docker started the process of building the container image as specified in the docker file. If you check the available images, you will see your brand-new container image:

```
PS C:\MyApp> docker images
REPOSITORY                                  TAG
IMAGE ID          CREATED          SIZE
myappimage                                  v1
78fd07b50870      3 minutes ago    5.15GB
mcr.microsoft.com/windows/servercore/iis    windowsservercore-ltsc2019
1dfea62c25d8      5 weeks ago      5.15GB
mcr.microsoft.com/windows/servercore        ltsc2019
fdf6432edbdc      5 weeks ago      4.94GB
```

Now let's test our image and the application inside of it:

```
PS C:\MyApp> docker run -d -p 8080:80 --name mycontainer myappimage:v1
e7174997fc65c0d5e9da62eddf3b6df4c6b5f77c6dd049baef0030963ef3442c
```

The preceding command is also similar to previous examples. It uses docker run to create and start a new container, runs it detached or as a service, maps port 8080 of the host to the container, names the container as "mycontainer", and uses the previously created container image as base. Now let's check if the container is running properly:

```
PS C:\MyApp> docker ps
CONTAINER ID        IMAGE               COMMAND
CREATED             STATUS              PORTS                       NAMES
e7174997fc65        myappimage:v1       "C:\\ServiceMonitor.e…"
2 minutes ago       Up 2 minutes        0.0.0.0:8080->80/tcp    mycontainer
```

As you can see from the output, all good with the container. So now, let's open a browser and open `http://localhost:8080/myapp.html` to check if the application is running.

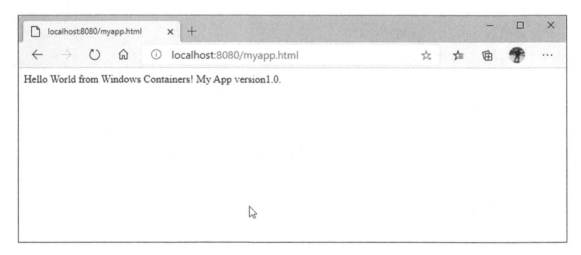

Figure 2-6. *Sample application on web browser*

As you can see in Figure 2-6, our application is working properly. If you started this book with no knowledge on Windows Container, you should be proud of yourself now! You have a fully functioning container image, and that can be redeployed over and over with an application that you tested and works fine.

Now let's pick it up a notck. Let's image a situation – very common in DevOps scenarios – where an update to the application was made and you need to deploy a new version of it. To emulate that in our example, we will make an update to the myapp.html file. Using Notepad, let's update the text in the file to

```
Hello World from the awesome Windows Containers platform! My App version2.0.
```

Once you update the file, save it and close Notepad. Now, let's update the image.

Here's a question for you: How do you do that? Before you read the following information, give it a try. Remember the previous chapter and sections. See if you can do that without checking the following information.

Ready to try it? So, here's the catch – we won't update the container image. What we will do is to build a new image from the same source, with the same docker file, same name, but different tag. Back in our elevated PowerShell session, let's run the docker build command again with slightly different option:

```
PS C:\MyApp> docker build -t myappimage:v2 .
Sending build context to Docker daemon  3.072kB
Step 1/3 : FROM mcr.microsoft.com/windows/servercore/iis:windowsservercore-ltsc2019
 ---> 1dfea62c25d8
Step 2/3 : WORKDIR C:\\InetPub\\WWWRoot
 ---> Using cache
 ---> eac04660bd88
Step 3/3 : COPY . .
 ---> c09b67a5b39b
Successfully built c09b67a5b39b
Successfully tagged myappimage:v2
```

Notice we ran exactly the same command as the one before to build our container image with the only difference being the v2 option in the tag. Let's look at the available container images:

```
PS C:\MyApp> docker images
REPOSITORY                                TAG
IMAGE ID          CREATED          SIZE
myappimage                                v2
c09b67a5b39b      About a minute ago    5.15GB
```

```
myappimage                                    v1
78fd07b50870          26 minutes ago     5.15GB
mcr.microsoft.com/windows/servercore/iis     windowsservercore-ltsc2019
1dfea62c25d8          5 weeks ago        5.15GB
mcr.microsoft.com/windows/servercore         ltsc2019
fdf6432edbdc          5 weeks ago        4.94GB
```

We now have two versions of the container image: version 1 and version 2. If you think about it, it's very helpful to have the previous version there. If something goes wrong with the new version, you can safely revert back to the previous version. Also, the other important thing to notice here is that we did not change the docker file itself. The commands we used to tell docker how to build the container image are still the same – the only thing that changed was the application itself. So now let's run a new container with the new version of the application:

```
PS C:\MyApp> docker run -d -p 8081:80 --name mynewcontainer myappimage:v2
bd357b31538e1f4ea5775f8a7a608b5b1a08b3e0d148819104bcca52b723ebbc
```

Notice a few things changed from the previous docker run command we used. First, we had to change the port on the host from 8080 to 8081. That is simply because we still have the previous container running with the port 8080 mapped to it. If we had removed the previous container, that port would be available for us to use. The next thing we changed is the container name – same principle, you can't have two containers with the same name. Next, and the most important thing here, we use the version 2 of our container image. If we open another web browser session, we can check the application has been updated, as shown in Figure 2-7.

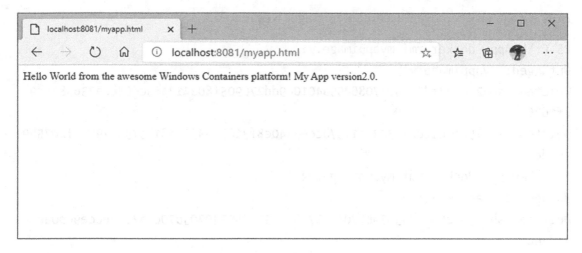

Figure 2-7. *Updated application from new container image*

Let's check the containers we have running now:

```
PS C:\MyApp> docker ps
CONTAINER ID          IMAGE               COMMAND                   CREATED
STATUS                PORTS                      NAMES
bd357b31538e          myappimage:v2          "C:\\ServiceMonitor.e…"   6 minutes
ago        Up 6 minutes          0.0.0.0:8081->80/tcp    mynewcontainer
e7174997fc65          myappimage:v1          "C:\\ServiceMonitor.e…"   30
minutes ago        Up 30 minutes          0.0.0.0:8080->80/tcp    mycontainer
```

The two versions of the application are running in different containers on this container host – each one in its own port. You can choose to remove the original container and keep the new one running now.

In preparation to our next chapter, let's clean up the environment. The first thing you want to do is to remove the containers. Remember, by default, you can't remove a running container, so we have to either stop the container or use the "-f" option:

```
PS C:\MyApp> docker rm mycontainer -f
mycontainer
PS C:\MyApp> docker rm mynewcontainer -f
mynewcontainer
```

Now we can also remove the container images we created:

```
PS C:\MyApp> docker rmi myappimage:v1
Untagged: myappimage:v1
Deleted: sha256:78fd07b5087086d95a4010e9dd270905f80a412af5c664eee2365874c9
cf1626
Deleted: sha256:5c12e223343fc1f57bcce5340c8f31639a3901b81857983792cef2075b9
99cdc
PS C:\MyApp> docker rmi myappimage:v2
Untagged: myappimage:v2
Deleted: sha256:c09b67a5b39b77044337c866f350c55540703b70e3a21ffecce9eb0aec
4f7464
Deleted: sha256:39f7ac66752812228b2fdb7a2147aefada868ab7fced36e55122cea9ef9
3b9ad
Deleted: sha256:eac04660bd88db2949aa05cc1b9d5e8b3b8b419ae570a184b72c5325f3d
bc1b7
Deleted: sha256:0cb04ef95308c800e77975f562537b08d8f2008a8522d40083ddac2231d
f1eb2
```

Notice how each deleted image has only its own layers deleted. The base image used to create our container images – the IIS image layers – is still there.

Hopefully, you now have a way better understanding on how Windows Containers work, and you are feeling more comfortable and confident. In the next chapters, we will start exploring more complex scenarios, complex applications, and some best practices.

CHAPTER 3

Containerizing existing applications

So far, we looked at how containers work in general, how Docker is a key component in the containers space, and how to get started with containers on Windows. One of the key aspects of containers in the Windows space, however, is that most companies looking into adopting it are looking for ways to modernize their existing applications. Windows has been extremely successful as a platform for all kinds of applications, but most IT Pros today face a very complex challenge: How do they keep the lights on for their existing applications while modernizing their infrastructure?

Here's the problem: you have applications that were developed years ago, and while these applications are still running in production, the version of your server might be going out of support. In January of 2020 (just a few months before the writing of this book), Windows Servers 2008 and 2008 R2 reached their support lifecycle. Think about it; it's Windows Server 2008 – this book being written in 2020. Think about how many new things happened during this time, how many new technologies came up, and more importantly how the security landscape changed since then. Moving away from older versions of Windows Server is not just a need – it's a must. Now, the conversation about upgrading from older versions of Windows Server is not an easy one, and my intention with this book is not to convince you that you should upgrade, but help you in the process once you decide to upgrade. What I mean here is that there are multiple reasons your company might not be upgrading to more newer versions – lack of support from vendors/ISVs, lack of knowledge, lack of resources, and so many other reasons. These are all valid reasons, and from Microsoft, we provide multiple resources to help with that.

Specifically for containers, the process of containerizing an application today is not completely straightforward. Here's the thing: if an application works on Windows Servers 2016 and 2019 and it meets the criteria for containers (no GUI, runs on Server Core, etc.), there's a high chance, but not 100% certainty, that it's going to work on a Windows

© Vinicius Ramos Apolinario 2021
V. Ramos Apolinario, *Windows Containers for IT Pros*, https://doi.org/10.1007/978-1-4842-6686-1_3

Container. Furthermore, if an application is running on Windows Server 2008/2008 R2, there's a chance it will work on newer versions of Windows Server, but not 100% guaranteed. So, our option today to modernize an existing application is to first ensure this application works on Windows Server 2016 or 2019 and then validate if it runs on a container. Unfortunately, there's no direct path from Windows Server 2008 or Windows Server 2012 to a Windows container on Windows Server 2016 or 2019. In this chapter, we will look at the multiple aspects of containerizing an existing application with Windows containers, starting from the process of exporting the application to multiple variations of what the app might require from the OS.

Validating and exporting your application

The first step in containerizing an application is to identify what source you have. Regardless on the type of the application, you need to identify what are the artifacts you have in hand. For example: If the application was developed in house, you might have the source code. If the application was developed by an ISV, you might have the installer of this application. If the application is currently running on a server and you don't have the installation neither the source code, you still might be able to export the application. The main point here is that you need to identify how you are going to take the application and package it in a container. Let's look at a few options.

IIS web application

The first scenario we're going to analyze is an application that is currently deployed in a web server. One of the most common Windows scenarios are web applications running .Net Framework ASP.Net on IIS. There are hundreds of thousands of companies out there with this configuration. While some still have developers to update the code to .Net Core, in many cases, these apps are not maintained by devs anymore, so it's up to the IT Pro to export the application out of the running server. There are two main ways to do this.

Manually exporting an application from IIS

I should make a huge disclaimer here that this first option is error-prone and not recommended really, but I still wanted to showcase it as it can be a good learning experience when going through the process in real life. For this example, we will use a sample application that was developed for demonstration purposes. The application is currently hosted on my GitHub repository here: https://github.com/vrapolinario/ViniBeer. Here is a view of the application on a Windows Server 2008 R2 machine running IIS.

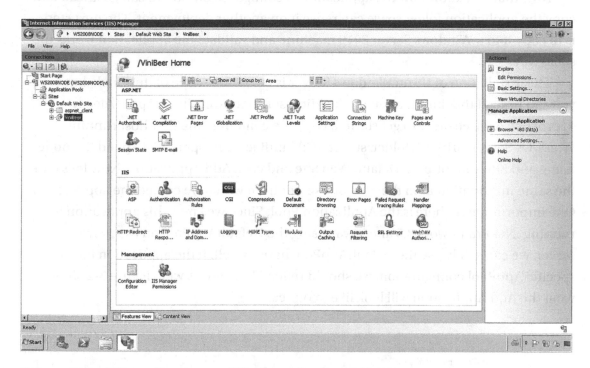

Figure 3-1. *IIS application on Windows Server 2008 R2*

As Figure 3-1 shows, this application was deployed on a Windows Server 2008 R2 host and is currently running under the Default Web Site. The application is an ASP.Net application developed using .Net Framework 3.5 – a common framework for the 2008 R2 era. The goal here is to extract this application from this machine and have it deployed on another host to validate the application works correctly. In the case of this particular application, there are no major secrets on how it works. There's no DB connection or anything else – which would make the process way complex. In this case, all we have to do is to check if the application has any particular configuration we might want to replicate. For that, we need to check the folder on which the application is hosted and if the application has any particular configuration in terms of IIS Application Pool that you might need to replicate. To check these configurations, right-click the application name (ViniBeer) and click Manage Application ➤ Advanced Settings. This will show you both the Application Pool and Physical Path. With this information, you have the necessary information for a simple application such as this one. Again, more complex scenarios will require checking many other things. We'll cover more complex configurations in the next section.

Now that you know how the application is configured on IIS, we can go ahead and copy the application folder so we can reuse it on another deployment. The next step is to copy it to a Windows Server 2019 machine and validate the application works the same way.

The installation of IIS on Windows Server is out of the scope of this book, but you can find all that information on the Microsoft Docs website: `https://docs.microsoft.com/en-us/`. To get started, copy the content to the new host running Windows Server 2019 to a folder, such as C:\ViniBeer, and open IIS. Expand the node name and Sites. Right-click Default Web Site and click Add Application. Now let's enter the same information as in the previous server from which we copied the application. One important item here is the Application Pool. Since we know this application is running .Net Framework 3.5 and it was using the DefaultAppPool on the previous server, we can safely use the DefaultAppPool here as well. If the application had a specific AppPool configuration, we should reflect that here as well. Figure 3-2 shows what the Add Application will look like in our case.

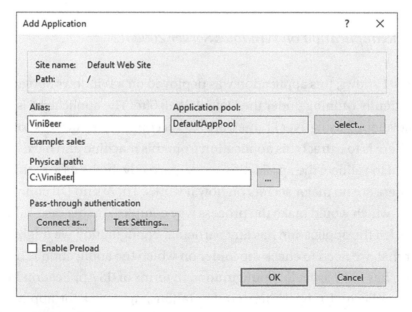

Figure 3-2. *Add Application on IIS on Windows Server 2019*

Since this is a very simple application, running the preceding process will effectively deploy our application. To validate the application works as expected, open a web browser and navigate to the website.

Figure 3-3. *ViniBeer application works on Windows Server 2019*

As you can see in Figure 3-3, the application works just fine on Windows Server 2019. We can now go ahead and create a docker file to go through the same steps we just went manually.

As you can probably remember from the previous chapters, we'll be building our docker file on the container host, so the first thing you need to do is to copy the application folder – the same one you copied to C:\ViniBeer previously – to your container host. To make it easier, let's copy to the same folder on the container host. Now, go ahead and create a dockerfile on the same folder and open it with Notepad.

At this point, you have an idea of what you need to do. Let's recap what we did on the Windows Server 2019 machine to make the website work:

1. We installed Windows Server 2019 and IIS with the necessary features to support ASP.Net.

2. We copied the application folder to C:\ViniBeer.

3. We added a new application to IIS mapping to our application folder using the DefaultAppPool.

Now, let's translate this to a dockerfile:

```
FROM mcr.microsoft.com/windows/servercore/iis:windowsservercore-ltsc2019
WORKDIR /ViniBeer
COPY . .
RUN PowerShell Install-WindowsFeature NET-Framework-45-ASPNET; \
    Install-WindowsFeature Web-Asp-Net45; \
    Import-Module WebAdministration; \
    New-WebApplication "ViniBeer" -Site 'Default Web Site' \
    -ApplicationPool "DefaultAppPool" -PhysicalPath "C:\ViniBeer"
```

As you know, the first line is calling our Windows base image, which in this case is the LTSC version of Windows Server 2019 with IIS. Next, we have our working directory, which is set to C:\ViniBeer. After that, we are copying the content from the context of the host to the context of the container image.

Finally, we get to the point on which manual steps we did on Windows Server 2019 are represented by PowerShell commands. This is probably the most important point of this example: at the end of the day, since containers don't have an UI, you have to translate whatever you do on the UI to a PowerShell cmdlet.

In the preceding example, before we go line by line, notice that we have the backslash character "\" at the end of each line. This ensures we're running all commands on the same layer, making our container image smaller than if we ran each command on a different RUN line.

The first line of the preceding RUN command installs the .Net Framework feature on Windows Server and is followed by the IIS sub-feature to install ASP.Net. Next, we use Import-Module to load the PowerShell module and be able to add the application to IIS, which is exactly what the last line does. Here, two notes are important.

First, note that the 'Default Web Site' is the only value for a parameter that has single quotes, rather than double quotes. Although PowerShell would usually accept double quotes, the docker file itself gets lost if you have a value represented with double quotes and a space in between. To avoid escaping the value, use single quotes for these cases. The second thing to notice is that we're not creating a new AppPool, just like in the previous example on Windows Server 2019, but you could add any other necessary command to prepare IIS for your application.

Now that we have the docker file configured, we can go ahead and build the image. On the container host, open an elevated PowerShell console and navigate to the application folder. Then run the docker build command:

```
PS C:\ViniBeer> docker build -t vinibeerimage:v1 .
Sending build context to Docker daemon   9.78MB
Step 1/4 : FROM mcr.microsoft.com/windows/servercore/iis:windowsservercore-
ltsc2019
 ---> 1dfea62c25d8
Step 2/4 : WORKDIR /ViniBeer
 ---> Running in f43da98ac9f2
Removing intermediate container f43da98ac9f2
 ---> 7545373284ce
Step 3/4 : COPY . .
 ---> 316467c9aa36
Step 4/4 : RUN PowerShell Install-WindowsFeature NET-Framework-45-
ASPNET;      Install-WindowsFeature Web-Asp-Net45;   Import-Module
WebAdministration;   New-WebApplication "ViniBeer" -Site 'Default Web
Site' -ApplicationPool "DefaultAppPool" -PhysicalPath "C:\ViniBeer"
 ---> Running in 6e3b4930b232

Success Restart Needed Exit Code    Feature Result
------- -------------- ---------    --------------
True    No             Success      {ASP.NET 4.7}
True    No             Success      {Application Development, ASP.NET
                                    4.7,...

Path            : /ViniBeer
ApplicationPool : DefaultAppPool
EnabledProtocols : http
PhysicalPath    : C:\ViniBeer
```

```
Removing intermediate container 6e3b4930b232
 ---> b257bfdef42d
Successfully built b257bfdef42d
Successfully tagged vinibeerimage:v1
```

The preceding output shows each step the docker build command went through to build our container image. Notice that it reflects nicely with our previous manual process, but with PowerShell.

Now the final test: Run a new container based on this image to ensure the application works correctly. For that, let's run the docker run command:

```
PS C:\ViniBeer> docker run -d -p 8080:80 --name vinibeercontainer
vinibeerimage:v1
91d183462718d47e19c0455499f9e564c5d2a78b587ac82daeb62b33816e83bc
```

With the previous command executed successfully, let's open a browser and check the application.

Figure 3-4. Web application working on a container

The application in Figure 3-4 works as expected, but more importantly note the URL. We're pointing to the port mapped on the docker run command to the port 80 of the container. We now have a fully functioning version of our application hosted on a container image on which we can instantiate at any time in any environment.

Yes, I know you are thinking that not all applications are that easy to deploy on IIS. The application you might be thinking on containerizing might have multiple specific configurations on IIS, a database connection, and many other dependencies. The reason we went through the preceding scenario is for you to understand the process. From here, we can containerize anything we want – as long as it is supported on a Windows Container – we just have to provide the configuration for our application on the docker file. Now let's look at another option that will make your life much easier.

Exporting an IIS application with Web Deploy

Here's an expert advice: whenever you have a tool to automate a process, use that tool. Exporting the application from IIS manually is nowhere near effective as using Web Deploy. Web Deploy is a Microsoft tool to manage IIS applications. It was launched many years ago with the intention to help administrators manage their IIS instances, and it's a great tool if you have to export an application from one server and import on another one.

Web Deploy can be installed on your Windows Server 2008 R2 to export the application and also installed on a Windows Server 2019 to import the same application, so the validation process we covered in the previous section is still valid – but way easier.

For more information on how to install and use Web Deploy, check out the Microsoft documentation page: `https://docs.microsoft.com/en-us/iis/install/installing-publishing-technologies/installing-and-configuring-web-deploy-on-iis-80-or-later`.

In our example, we'll use the same application and start with the Windows Server 2019 host on which we validated the application does work on the latest OS. Once you install Web Deploy, open IIS Manager and navigate to the application. Right-click the application ViniBeer, and you'll notice a new option shows up on the menu: Deploy ➤ Export Application.

When you open that option, you'll notice that Web Deploy will help you in the process of exporting not just the application itself but all the configuration for that application.

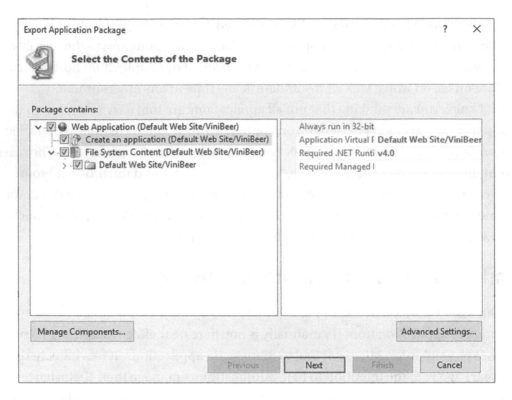

Figure 3-5. *Web Deploy export process*

As you can see in Figure 3-5, Web Deploy already identified all the components necessary for this application – not just in terms of the application configuration on IIS, but the folder content as well. If this application had any additional configuration, such as SQL database connection string, Web Deploy would catch that and include in the preceding screen. If we move on with the wizard, we'll be asked for any additional parameters we'd like to add and next the location to store the ZIP file on which the application export will be hosted. You can save the file in a location on which you'll be able to copy to your container host.

The process, however, to import this on an environment such as a container – or Server Core for that matter – is a bit different, though. Here's what the process looks like:

1. Install Windows Server 2019 and IIS with the necessary features to support ASP.Net.

2. Copy the exported zip file to C:\ViniBeer.

3. Add the Web Deploy PowerShell snap-in so we can run the Web Deploy commands on a PowerShell session.

4. Import the zip file via Web Deploy cmdlet using all the default.

With this said, let's look at what a docker file would look like:

```
FROM mcr.microsoft.com/dotnet/framework/aspnet:4.8-windowsservercore-
ltsc2019
WORKDIR /ViniBeer
COPY ViniBeer.zip .
RUN PowerShell Invoke-WebRequest https://download.microsoft.com/
download/0/1/D/01DC28EA-638C-4A22-A57B-4CEF97755C6C/WebDeploy_amd64_en-US.
msi -OutFile ./webdeploy.msi; \
    Start-Process msiexec -Wait -ArgumentList '/I C:\DockerDemo\webdeploy.
    msi /quiet /NoRestart /passive ADDLOCAL=ALL LicenseAccepted="0"'; \
    Add-PSSnapin WDeploySnapin3.0; \
    Restore-WDPackage -Package C:\ViniBeer\ViniBeer.zip
```

First, one thing you should know: in the previous example, we used the IIS image and then installed the necessary ASP.Net components. This is actually not necessary since Microsoft does provide an ASP.Net image with IIS already configured. So, in this case, we used the ASP.Net 4.8 image from Windows Server 2019 Server Core.

Then we created our working directory at C:\ViniBeer. Next, we copied only the zip file to that folder, since the zip file has everything we need.

For the PowerShell portion – which represents manual steps we'd have to perform – we started by downloading the Web Deploy binary using the Invoke-WebRequest and saved it as webdeploy.msi on the same ViniBeer folder. Next, we used the Start-Process to launch msiexec, which installs msi files. The parameters for installing Web Deploy via command line are documented on the Web Deploy docs page we provided earlier. After that, we added the Web Deploy snap-in. This is necessary as we installed Web Deploy and we need to use the PowerShell cmdlets on the same PowerShell console we're in. With the snap-in added, we can then use the Restore-WDPackage command with the location of the zip file we wanted to import. With the docker file ready, we can run the docker build command:

```
PS C:\ViniBeer> docker build -t webdeployimage:v1 .
Sending build context to Docker daemon  579.6kB
```

```
Step 1/4 : FROM mcr.microsoft.com/dotnet/framework/aspnet:4.8-
windowsservercore-ltsc2019
 ---> 14f860902b49
Step 2/4 : WORKDIR /DockerDemo
 ---> Running in 459ddcd246b6
Removing intermediate container 459ddcd246b6
 ---> 763b6400597a
Step 3/4 : COPY . .
 ---> 212d99e65d9a
Step 4/4 : RUN Invoke-WebRequest https://download.microsoft.com/
download/0/1/D/01DC28EA-638C-4A22-A57B-4CEF97755C6C/WebDeploy_
amd64_en-US.msi -OutFile ./webdeploy.msi;        Start-Process
msiexec -Wait -ArgumentList '/I C:\DockerDemo\webdeploy.msi /quiet /
NoRestart /passive ADDLOCAL=ALL LicenseAccepted="0"';  Add-PSSnapin
WDeploySnapin3.0;  Restore-WDPackage -Package .\DockerDemoWebsite.zip
 ---> Running in 11d2d3f52e0f

Package            : C:\DockerDemo\DockerDemoWebsite.zip
Auto               :
TimeTaken          : 0:2
Errors             : 0
Warnings           : 0
BytesCopied        : 1774413
ObjectsDeleted     : 0
ObjectsUpdated     : 1
ObjectsAdded       : 133
TotalChanges       : 134
ParameterChanges : 0
```

We now have an image ready to go with our web application. We can use the same docker run commands we used before to run an instance of our application – which in this case preserves all the complex IIS configurations from the server on which it was exported.

MSI application

The next type of common application we'll cover are MSI packaged applications. There's a caveat here, though: MSI applications might be applications that are simply installed and you call the application when needed, or they might be applications that run on the background as a Windows service. The first option requires only that you know how to install the application using PowerShell. The second kind requires that you know how to install the MSI package via PowerShell and that you know the service itself so you can instantiate it as an entry point in your docker file. As you remember, containers will only run detached – or in the background – if a service is instantiated as an entry point. If your MSI application is going to run as a service inside the container, then you need to instantiate it – otherwise, the container will exit as there's nothing to run.

MSI packages for non-service applications

The example we will use in this book is only an example of how you'd go with installing an MSI package that deploys something to your container image that can then be used later. For our example, we will use the MSI package that deploys Azure CLI. Azure CLI is a command-line tool that allows you to manage Azure resources from Shell interfaces, such as PowerShell. The caveat here is that although you can install this tool on a Server Core machine, it does not work on a Windows container as it does require some APIs not available on Windows containers today. However, since our goal here is just to show how an MSI package that does not run as a service is installed, we will go ahead and use that for exercise, so you can replicate in a test environment. Here is the docker file for installing the Azure CLI MSI package:

```
FROM mcr.microsoft.com/windows/servercore:ltsc2019
RUN powershell Invoke-WebRequest -Uri https://aka.ms/installazurecliwindows
-OutFile .\AzureCLI.msi; Start-Process msiexec.exe -Wait -ArgumentList '/I
AzureCLI.msi /quiet'; rm .\AzureCLI.msi
```

Notice that our docker file is extremely simple and short. The first line starts bringing the Server Core container image, and the next line is already the installation of the MSI package. This is possible because we are downloading the package from the Web. If in your case the MSI package was hosted on your container host, the docker file would look like this:

```
FROM mcr.microsoft.com/windows/servercore:ltsc2019
WORKDIR ./AzureCLI
```

```
COPY AzureCLI.msi .
RUN powershell Start-Process msiexec.exe -Wait -ArgumentList '/I AzureCLI.
msi /quiet'
```

The second option creates a working directory to copy the MSI package to then install the file. Notice that regardless of the option we're using, the installation of the MSI package is still the same. We can now go ahead and use docker build to create a new container image with our application installed.

MSI packages for background service applications

This type of application is a bit more complex to containerize, but still possible. In the previous section, we covered the installation of an MSI package and that will still be necessary, but now we need to add something else: the entry point of the service you want to instantiate. More important than that, actually, is we need something to be instantiated to watch that service. Unfortunately, there's no generic tool for that. If you recall from Chapter 1, we covered a tool used on the IIS image called Service Monitor. That tool was created by the IIS team to monitor the state of the IIS service (w3svc) and exit if the status of that service enters a different state than "started." For MSI packages that deploy a service that runs on the background, you could use the same tool and point to your service.

Here's my recommendation on what to do before you think about containerizing your application:

1. Deploy your application on a Windows Server 2019 Server Core server using PowerShell. This will ensure your application is correctly deployed – just like in the previous section.

2. On the Server Core image, run the Get-Service command to identify the name of the service that was deployed – in case you don't know already. With this information, we can use the Service Monitor tool to monitor the state of the service and have an entry point in our docker file.

With the preceding recommendation completed, let's look into what the steps on a docker file would look like:

1. Start from Server Core or a specific image that meets your needs.

2. Set up the working directory so we can copy the MSI file later.

3. Copy the MSI file to the container image.

4. Use the Start-Process cmdlet to initiate msiexec and install the application.

5. Download the Service Monitor tool.

6. Set the entry point to Service Monitor and target the service deployed in the previous step.

With all this said, let's take a look at a sample docker file:

```
FROM mcr.microsoft.com/dotnet/framework/runtime:4.8
WORKDIR /MyApp
COPY Application.msi .
RUN powershell Start-Process msiexec.exe -Wait -ArgumentList '/I C:\MyApp\
Application.msi /quiet /qn'; \
    Invoke-WebRequest -UseBasicParsing -Uri "https://dotnetbinaries.
    blob.core.windows.net/servicemonitor/2.0.1.10/ServiceMonitor.exe"
    -OutFile "C:\ServiceMonitor.exe" ENTRYPOINT ["C:\\ServiceMonitor.exe",
    "ApplicationService"]
```

Let's start by looking at the very first line that, as you know, calls out the base image to be used. In the case of the preceding example, we are using the .Net Framework runtime image. The reason I decided to use this image is because I know that my application was built on .Net Framework, so we need the components installed. I could start from the Server Core image and add the components, but as we discussed previously, we know we can skip that by using an official image.

The next two lines are very straightforward, and we used before. Basically, what we are doing is setting the working directory and copying the application MSI file.

After that, we call out the PowerShell cmdlet Start-Process to install the MSI file – which is not different from what we did before. The next step is, though.

Along with the Start-Process command, we embedded another PowerShell command in the same RUN action. As you remember, this is a best practice to make the image smaller. The command we run here is the Invoke-WebRequest to download the Service Monitor executable and save it in the C:\ drive.

The final line is a new one for us: the "ENTRYPOINT". As explained before, containers need something specified as an entry point – otherwise, the container will exit its start state and stop. The application we installed runs on the background as a

Windows Service, so we need the Service Monitor executable to be set as entry point. The semantics of the entry point line here is to call out the executable and its parameters. In our case, the executable is on the C:\ drive, and you'll notice we had to use the double backslash to reflect how the docker file is read. We then passed the name of the service as we gathered when we tested the application on a regular Server Core installation.

We can now go ahead and build the image:

```
PS C:\MyApp> docker build -t msiimage:v1 .
Sending build context to Docker daemon  69.89MB
Step 1/5 : FROM mcr.microsoft.com/dotnet/framework/runtime:4.8
 ---> 149f2e4abbde
Step 2/5 : WORKDIR /MyApp
 ---> Running in e363bc9340c9
Removing intermediate container e363bc9340c9
 ---> b91074967765
Step 3/5 : COPY Application.msi .
 ---> 2e724ff3c1be
Step 4/5 : RUN powershell Start-Process msiexec.exe -Wait -ArgumentList '/I
C:\MyApp\Application.msi /quiet /qn';   Invoke-WebRequest -UseBasicParsing
-Uri "https://dotnetbinaries.blob.core.windows.net/servicemonitor/2.0.1.10/
ServiceMonitor.exe" -OutFile "C:\ServiceMonitor.exe"
 ---> Running in faf362dbde4e
Removing intermediate container faf362dbde4e
 ---> 3756afadb504
Step 5/5 : ENTRYPOINT ["C:\\ServiceMonitor.exe", "ApplicationService"]
 ---> Running in ecb46b058199
Removing intermediate container ecb46b058199
 ---> b1e8c651f5f7
Successfully built b1e8c651f5f7
Successfully tagged msiimage:v1
```

We can also run a new container based on the image we just created:

```
PS C:\MyApp> docker run -d -p 8080:443 --name msicontainer msiimage:v1
d089c78092134709be0190b16be617152add82f60e34a697b1d4601f67b619fa
```

The preceding command is not new – the only difference from previously used docker run examples is that in this case we know the application is listening on port 443. If we run the docker ps command now, you can see that the container image is running:

```
PS C:\MyApp> docker ps -a
CONTAINER ID        IMAGE                COMMAND                   CREATED
STATUS              PORTS                  NAMES
d089c7809213        msiimage:v1          "C:\\ServiceMonitor.e…"   2 seconds
ago      Up 1 second         0.0.0.0:8080->443/tcp   msicontainer
```

I hope these examples give you an idea on how you go by exporting your application and importing it inside a container. These are the most common types of existing applications being containerized today. In the real world, your application will have specific dependencies and specific characteristics. However, the main takeaway from this process is that regardless of how you are going to export the application from your current server to a container, passing those to the docker file is pretty much as passing PowerShell commands as if you were performing the tasks on a Server Core machine.

Active Directory authentication with group Managed Service Accounts

This might have crossed your mind as we went through the examples in the previous section: What about applications that authenticate against Active Directory (AD)? Can I domain-join a container?

The short answer to the preceding question is that you can't domain-join a container. There is, however, an alternative to have applications running inside a container to be able to authenticate against an Active Directory Domain Controller.

Let's look at a scenario to clarify what the preceding statement means: if you have a web application that authenticates your user when you access it, your developer might have integrated the authentication of said web application with AD to provide a Single Sign-On experience – or even to simply use AD as the authentication mechanism, even if Single Sign-On is not provided. The way it works outside of containers is something like this:

Traditionally, when a user accesses a domain-joined resource and an authentication is required, the application – in this case a website – will query the Active Directory to validate the credentials. Once authenticated, the web application will check the access the account will have based on its groups or directly provided authorization. Since the web application is running on a machine that is domain-joined, the process is very straightforward, and in fact, for cases such as IIS, this is all native and the only thing the developer had to do was to flag that the authentication was going to be Windows-based.

For the case of Containers, the container itself is not domain-joined, but the container host might be. In fact, for the following scenario to work, the container host must be domain-joined. Here's a diagram of the preceding scenario, but with containers:

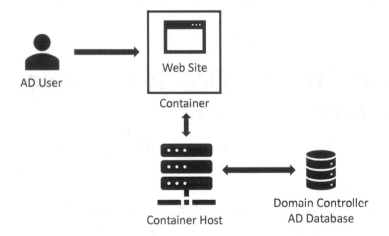

In the case of containers, the computer account used to communicate with Active Directory is not from the container itself, but from the container host. That's why the container host must be domain-joined. In addition to this, the process is not as straightforward as the traditional model. For containers, we use an AD resource called group Managed Service Accounts (gMSA). The notion of service accounts is not new to AD and is traditionally used for cases such as Network Load Balancers on which multiple authentications for a resource come from a distributed system (multiple nodes) but appear to come from a single resource. In those cases, the service principal used to authenticate must use the same account and password, so we use service accounts to solve that issue. In the case of containers, we use the service account on the host to authenticate any container running on top of it.

To get started on configuring gMSA there, just make sure you have at least one Windows Server 2012 Domain Controller (DC) on your domain. In order to add a Windows Server 2012 DC, you would have to prepare the domain to receive such Windows Server version as a DC, so AD would be prepared to operate the msDS-GroupManagedServiceAccount object type. However, there's no minimal functional level for domain or forest, which is already a relief for many enterprise customers who can't move to higher domain or forest functional level. The other requirement to get started is that you have the appropriate AD permission, which in this case is that you are part of the domain admin group or that you have delegation to create the preceding object type. You can find more details on how gMSA works on AD in general here: https://docs.microsoft.com/en-us/windows-server/security/group-managed-service-accounts/getting-started-with-group-managed-service-accounts.

To get started with gMSA, the first thing we need to do is to prepare our AD domain by creating a Key Distribution Service (KDS) root key. What we need to understand about it is that different from our regular user accounts, service accounts don't have an actual person to change the password from time to time. In this case, the KDS will be responsible for rotating the password for the service accounts available in the domain and releasing it to the authorized hosts, so they know the password they should use to authenticate changed.

To create a new KDS root key, run the following PowerShell cmdlet using a domain admin account (or an account with delegated rights) on a machine that has the AD PowerShell tools installed:

```
PS C:\> Add-KdsRootKey -EffectiveImmediately
```

Because the synchronization of all DCs is necessary before you can start using a service account, it is recommended that you wait 10 hours to ensure all DCs have the new information replicated.

Once the replication is completed, you can create a new service account. This process is composed of multiple steps in which you'll create a regular AD security group and then associate a service account to that security group, to then add the computer account of the container hosts to the security group:

```
PS C:\> New-ADGroup -Name "My Web Application" -SamAccountName "WebAppSG"
-GroupScope DomainLocal
```

The preceding command should not be strange to you if you ever managed AD via PowerShell. This is a regular cmdlet used to create a new security group called My Web Application on which the group account name is WebAppSG and the scope is of the local domain. Next, we can create a new service account:

```
PS C:\> New-ADServiceAccount -Name "MyWebApp" -DnsHostName "mywebapp.
vinibeer.local" -ServicePrincipalNames "host/MyWebApp", "host/mywebapp.
vinibeer.local" -PrincipalsAllowedToRetrieveManagedPassword "WebAppSG"
```

The preceding command is a bit more complex if you are not familiar with service accounts. In fact, even if you are, it does have some unique aspects to it because of the nature of containers. The command starts by attributing a name to our service account. Then we provide the DNS name that will be used for authentication – for example, if the users access the website via mywebapp.vinibeer.local, then we need to register that DNS name. Next, we add the service principals (SP). The thing here is that a regular domain-joined machine would register its SP, but since containers are not domain-joined, we need to manually add them here. We added all names that might be needed for authentication, such as the service group and the DNS name. Next, we provided the name of the security group created in the previous step as the one allowed to retrieve the managed password, so any host on that group can retrieve the password. Here, we should make a note that dealing with service accounts and managed password must be something you design really well to avoid non-authorized hosts to access the managed password if they don't have to. Keep in mind you should try to add just the necessary hosts to a service account and service accounts should be created with a minimal authorization scope. Next, we need to add the hosts to the security group:

```
PS C:\> Add-ADGroupMember -Identity "MyWebApp" -Members "Host1$", "Host2$",
"Host3$"
```

The preceding command is also a regular cmdlet used in AD management. It simply adds the container hosts' computer accounts to the security group we created earlier. Now that we configured the AD side, we can move to the configuration on the container host.

On your container host, the first recommended thing to do is to validate if the host can retrieve the service account and its managed password. To do that, we can run the following command:

```
PS C:\> Test-ADServiceAccount -Identity MyWebApp
```

```
True
```

The result of the preceding command returns true if the computer is able to retrieve the managed password successfully. If you get that same result, you can move to the next step.

In terms of container host configuration, the final step needed is to create a credential specification JSON file. This is necessary as we don't want to change the code in the application in order to map which gMSA the container will use to authenticate. By default, Docker will look for a credential spec on C:\ProgramData\Docker\ CredentialSpecs on each container host. If you have multiple container hosts that will run this container, the following process can be performed on the first container host, and then you can copy the file to the next ones. To create a new credential spec, run the following on a container host:

```
PS C:\> Install-Module CredentialSpec
PS C:\> New-CredentialSpec -AccountName MyWebApp
```

The preceding commands will install the Credential Spec PowerShell module and then create a new credential spec file on the default docker directory. You can now copy this file from this container host and reuse it on additional container hosts that might host a container that will spin up an instance of your application. This finalizes the configuration necessary on our container host. Now, we need to configure the application to use gMSA. That process will be different depending on the type of application you want to use inside the container.

Web applications on gMSA

For web applications on IIS, we need to set up each application pool to use a specific identity. By default, the Default Application Pool will use the ApplicationPoolIdentity, and we need to change that to Network Service. To do that, we'll use an IIS command-line tool (keep in mind that this process is a regular IIS process and usually done through the GUI; since containers don't have a GUI, we'll use the command line). The following command can be added to your docker file:

```
RUN %windir%\system32\inetsrv\appcmd.exe set AppPool DefaultAppPool
-processModel.identityType:NetworkService
```

The preceding command uses the appcmd.exe which is the native command-line tool to manage IIS outside of PowerShell. The interesting thing here is that your container can move from dev, to test, to prod environments with no changes – as long as the container host is properly configured.

Windows service apps on gMSA

The same principal as web applications on IIS applies to Windows services: all you have to do is to change the account used to authenticate to use Network Service. To do that, you can add the following command to the docker file:

```
RUN sc.exe config "ServiceName" obj= "NT AUTHORITY\NETWORK SERVICE"
password= ""
```

Keep in mind that the preceding line has to be added after the commands in the docker file that install the application so the service is actually there to be changed.

Console applications on gMSA

For general applications that are not running on IIS or Windows services, you can actually change the context of the container itself, so it uses the Network Service. For that, you can add the following line to your docker file:

```
USER "NT AUTHORITY\NETWORK SERVICE"
```

Running containers with gMSA

The process for configuring gMSA is not as straightforward as simply marking a check box, so let's recap what we did so far:

1. We enabled KDS root key in our AD domain and waited 10 hours to ensure the replication was completed.

2. We created a security group and then a service account mapping the security group and then added the container hosts' computer accounts to the security group.

3. We created a credential spec in the first container host and copied the file to additional container hosts that will run an instance of our container.

4. Then we configured the docker file to run the application – either IIS, Windows service, or generic console app – with Network Service.

Now that all the preceding configuration is completed, we can run the container – but we still need to tell docker that the container will run with a different context:

```
PS C:\> docker run --security-opt "credentialspec=file://mywebapp_specfile.
json" --hostname mywebapp -d -p 8080:80 --name mycontainer mycontainerimage
```

With the preceding command, we now have a container running with an instance of our application on which gMSA is being used to authenticate our application. There are two new parameters in the preceding command that we did not cover yet.

The first one is the --security-opt which is the parameter that tells docker the container will use gMSA and passes which credential spec file to use. The next one is the --hostname parameter. This parameter actually has nothing to do with gMSA – it simply tells the container which hostname to use. If you're using Windows Server, version 1709 or 1803, this parameter is necessary and must match the gMSA SAM Account Name used previously. On recent releases of Windows Server, this parameter is not necessary, but the container will still end up using that name as identification.

Access to devices and GPU acceleration with Windows Containers

Before we start this section of the chapter, let's go back to Chapter 1 and remember a key concept with containers: containers have an isolation mode on which the goal is to isolate the application inside of a container from other containers and the host. While this isolation helps when something goes wrong with the container, it means the container – by default – won't have access to everything the host OS has. What that means is containers will have minimal access to hardware resources, what is considered enough for an OS and its application to work. If the application relies on additional hardware to work, we need to declare its dependencies at the moment the container is instantiated – the docker run command. There are some requirements to implement access to devices, though:

1. The container host must be running a version of Windows Server or Windows 10 post 1809. For Windows Server, that means Windows Server 2019 and above.

2. The container image must be post 1809 as well. For general devices, the container image can be a Server Core or Nano Server image, but for GPU acceleration, the image must be running the Windows image.

3. Device access is only available on process isolation mode. Device access is not supported on hypervisor isolation mode at the moment of the writing of this book.

4. The Docker engine version must be 19.03 or newer.

5. You need to identify which device you want to map to the container and its Interface Class GUID. A list of supported devices and its Interface Class GUID is available at `https://docs.microsoft.com/en-us/virtualization/windowscontainers/deploy-containers/hardware-devices-in-containers`.

As an example, to provide access to a COM port, we can run the following command:

```
PS C:\> docker run -d --device= class/86E0D1E0-8089-11D0-9CE4-08003E301F73
--name mycontainer myimage:v1
```

The --device option is the new item in the preceding command, and in this case, we pass the Interface Class GUID of a COM port, so the container can now access these devices. Keep in mind that device mapping is driver dependent, so if you try to map a device that is not supported, an unexpected behavior might happen. Additionally, we omitted the --isolation parameter from the preceding command because on Windows Server the default mode is process. If you run the preceding command on a Windows 10 container host, you need to modify the command a little bit:

```
PS C:\> docker run -d --isolation process --device= class/86E0D1E0-8089-
11D0-9CE4-08003E301F73 --name mycontainer myimage:v1
```

For GPU acceleration, the process is pretty much the same as the preceding one. However, as of the writing of this book, the support for GPU is actually tied to DirectX – not the GPU itself. This is because not only the device needs to be mapped but the container image OS needs the specific drivers of the devices being mapped and its components. For Windows Containers, while you can map a GPU, the components on the Windows container images are limited to using DirectX. In any case, DirectX is a technology that serves as an interface between application and GPU for processing. It's usually used by graphic applications such as games, but also for data processing on which high performance is necessary and CPU-based processing is not sufficient. One example of workloads running on containers that benefit from GPU acceleration are machine learning workloads.

Specifically for GPU/DirectX support, there is one additional requirement: that your GPU driver version is WDDM 2.5 or newer. You can check that information by running dxdiag.exe on your container host. The output of that executable will show you the detailed information about your display driver, as shown in Figure 3-6.

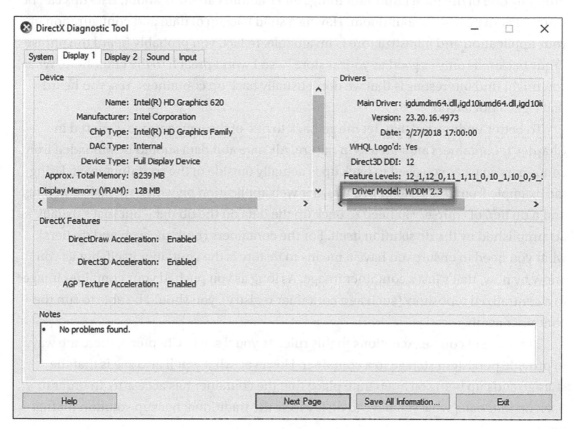

Figure 3-6. *DirectX diagnostic tool and display driver model*

If your driver shows as WDDM 2.5 or newer, you can run the following command:

```
PS C:\> docker run -d --device class/5B45201D-F2F2-4F3B-85BB-30FF1F953599
--name mycontainer mcr.microsoft.com/windows:1809
```

The preceding command is the same – in terms of structure – as the previous example. The main difference here is the device Interface Class GUID. The other difference you might notice is the Windows image. I left that base image on purpose to call out once again that specifically for GPU acceleration via DirectX you need to use the Windows base image rather than the Server Core or Nano Server ones. You can still build your own image based on the Windows image, but keep that in mind if you plan to use GPU acceleration.

Backup and Windows Containers

Probably one of the most important things an IT admin can think about, backups can be your ticket to heaven or your doom. Having a solid backup of data and configuration of your application and infrastructure is invaluable. In fact, you probably heard the phrase "Your backup is only as good as your restore" – so I won't preach to the choir here. What you might find interesting is that we don't usually back up containers. Yes, you heard that right – not a typo.

To better understand that, let me go back to one of the concepts we explored in Chapter 1: containers are stateless in nature. All state and data should be offloaded from containers so what you need to back up is actually outside of the container itself. Using the example from that chapter of a two-tier web application on which we have a web tier and a db tier, of course, you need to back up the data on the db tier – but that's usually accomplished by the db solution itself. For the containers (both the web and db tiers), what you need to ensure you have a means to restore is the container itself, but as you know by now, that's just a container image. As long as you pushed your container image to a centralized repository (such as a container registry), you should be able to run the container again.

There are of course exceptions to this rule. As you'll see in Chapter 4, there are ways to provide persistent storage to a container. However, what you'll also see is that the storage ends up being on a separate place that the container has access to. In order to back up that data, what you have to do is to use the traditional backup solution for that location.

On Linux, there's an option to use the docker commit command to create a "backup" of a running container, but that command is not available on Windows.

Keep in mind that this does not eliminate the need to back up your container host if that host is storing data the containers are using as well as if any other application is running alongside your containers.

Anti-virus and Windows Containers

If you've been managing VMware or Hyper-V hosts, you are probably familiar with the issues that virtualization brings to anti-virus (AV) solutions. Isolation from the host computer to the guest means the AV on the host is not able to fully scan the runtime of the isolated partition. In addition to that, cases on which multiple VMs access the same storage or file system end up having cases of double scan, which in turn results in lower performance and overutilization of resources. For server virtualization, the industry has solved the problem. However, since containers are a relatively new technology, there are still cases on which AV solutions will impact the performance of applications being instantiated.

In the case of containers, remember that whenever we create an image, we have a new layer each time a command is executed in the docker file. The way Windows implements this is via a container isolation filter that creates a virtual overlay of package layers. Containers using that specific image will then see that as a container volume. The isolation filter keeps a placeholder for containers accessing the container image and its path in the file system of the container host. This allows that multiple containers access the same container image. If a file is modified in a specific container and that placeholder is broken, the isolation filter performs an operation called copy-on-write that basically creates a new layer for that specific container.

The problem here is that this isolation filter is below the AV range, so the AV solution is unaware of the placeholders, but it is aware of the container volume. When multiple containers access the same layers, what ends up happening is that a performance degradation might happen if the AV solution does not implement a solution for this scenario.

Windows Server and Windows 10 come with an embedded AV solution called Windows Defender. Windows Defender has a mechanism in place to avoid performance degradation when Windows containers are running. There's no action needed if you use Windows Defender.

If you notice performance degradation in your environment and you suspect the reason is your AV solution, you can check the information in this page: `https://docs.microsoft.com/en-us/windows-hardware/drivers/ifs/anti-virus-optimization-for-windows-containers`. While there's no action from a user perspective, you can check how to implement the recommended approach with your AV vendor and implement that in your environment.

Windows Update and containers

Since we're in the topic of keeping Windows Containers secure, another important aspect is how we deal with Windows Updates for security fixes. As you recall from Chapter 1, containers were created with the idea that they are stateless and disposable, which means they will live for running a specific action and will be removed after that action is completed. Of course, for cases on which a web application is being served, there's still a need to run the container indefinitely, but when we look at container orchestrator (we'll cover a bit more in the final chapter), we cannot assume the same container will be hosting that application.

With the preceding context, and the fact that containers have a need for minimal management and high startup times, when we look at Windows Containers, a lot was removed to provide a smaller attack surface and faster performance. On the flip side of that, the servicing stack is not present on the Windows base images for containers. What that means is that you don't simply run a Windows Update when a new patch is available. Keep in mind that with containers, if you need to change something that will affect multiple instances that will run your application, you should actually be changing the container image, not the container instance. With that said, what Microsoft does is every month we update the base container images to reflect the new security update released that month. Before we dive into the details of containers specifically, let's recap how security updates are provided on Windows Updates.

As an IT Pro, this shouldn't come as news to you: every month Microsoft releases new security updates on what is called Patch Tuesday. This release happens every second Tuesday of the month and is also referred as a B release. The B comes from the fact of the second Tuesday of the month and is preceded by the month number. For example, in June you have the 6B patch, in July you have the 7B package, and so on. There are other patch releases in the month, but they usually don't contain security updates and are available for what is called seekers: which means you have to manually go to Windows Update and manually select the option to install that specific update. They are released in the following weeks after the B release and are called C and D, respectively, depending on the week. So in our example, June could have a 6B, a 6C, and a 6D patch, but the most important one for that month is definitely 6B.

The other thing about Windows Update is that a couple years ago Microsoft changed how these patches are released to a new cumulative model. What cumulative model means is if you install a new package, then you have all the fixes from previous packages. For example, if you installed the 6B package, you got the fixes of 5B, 4B, and so on. The same way, if you install the 7B package, you got the fixes from the 6B, 6C, and 6D. On a non-containerized environment, there are many tools to deal with Windows Updates, such as Group Policy Objects (GPO), Windows Server Update Services (WSUS), System Center Configuration Manager (SCCM), Microsoft Intune, and many more. You can use these tools to create a plan for Windows Updates for workstations or servers, test and production environments, or any other need your company might have.

For containers, because we don't have the servicing stack on the Windows image, you have to use the base image as reference. Your planning model should be focused on which images you use each month and how you are going to update the images and containers you have. In a production environment with applications that are comprised of multiple containers, you should always use the strategy of your container orchestrator to update the containers. Container orchestrators such as Kubernetes and Docker Swarm already have a built-in solution to update the containers supporting your application with no or minimal downtime for the application. The scope of this book is to focus on the Windows Container platform, so we'll use an example of a single container application for you to understand how the process works and how the platform is built.

As mentioned earlier, the base container images will be updated from Microsoft on the Microsoft Container Registry (MCR), which is the back-end hosting location you see from the Docker Hub page. If you pull an image – let's say the Server Core base container image – today and you create a new image based on that Server Core base image, once a new B package is out, the Server Core image is also updated. Here's the process you can do to keep your images updated.

Let's start by looking at the images itself:

```
PS C:\ > docker images
REPOSITORY                                      TAG
IMAGE ID            CREATED             SIZE
mcr.microsoft.com/windows/servercore            ltsc2019
fdf6432edbdc        2 months ago        4.94GB
```

As you can see, the image was created 2 months ago, which means that for sure a new security update was released, and this image is outdated. In fact, let's create a new container based on this image and open it interactively to check the OS version and the Knowledge Base (KB) articles applied:

```
PS C:\WAC Test> docker run --entrypoint powershell -it mcr.microsoft.com/
windows/servercore:ltsc2019
Windows PowerShell
Copyright (C) Microsoft Corporation. All rights reserved.

PS C:\> systeminfo /fo csv | ConvertFrom-Csv | select OS*, System*,
Hotfix* | Format-List

OS Name              : Microsoft Windows Server 2019 Datacenter
OS Version           : 10.0.17763 N/A Build 17763
OS Manufacturer      : Microsoft Corporation
OS Configuration     : Standalone Server
OS Build Type        : Multiprocessor Free
System Boot Time     : 6/10/2020, 11:31:53 AM
System Manufacturer  : LENOVO
System Model         : 20BTS05T00
System Type          : x64-based PC
System Directory     : C:\Windows\system32
System Locale        : en-us;English (United States)
Hotfix(s)            : 2 Hotfix(s) Installed.,[01]: KB4549947,[02]:
KB4549949
```

Earlier we created a new container with the minimal instructions to have the container running, and then we ran a PowerShell cmdlet to show some system information. We can see on the last line of the output which hotfixes were installed.

Now, let's run the docker pull command on the same Server Core image that we already pulled. What the command will do is to check if the layers we have in our container host match the updated image from MCR, and if there's any difference, the new layers will be pulled:

```
PS C:\> docker pull mcr.microsoft.com/windows/servercore:ltsc2019
ltsc2019: Pulling from windows/servercore
4612f6d0b889: Already exists
666079ee0460: Already exists
Digest: sha256:0594b3bb67e2b5e57ab4414d7ce012a72582a6094b04b536c421ea1a23b7e7c7
Status: Downloaded newer image for mcr.microsoft.com/windows/
servercore:ltsc2019
mcr.microsoft.com/windows/servercore:ltsc2019
```

The output of our docker pull command shows that our Server Core image had an update and the new image was downloaded. If we run the docker images again, we can now see the new image:

```
PS C:\WAC Test> docker images
REPOSITORY                                      TAG
IMAGE ID            CREATED             SIZE
mcr.microsoft.com/windows/servercore            ltsc2019
486def14a6bd        2 weeks ago         4.98GB
mcr.microsoft.com/windows/servercore            <none>
fdf6432edbdc        2 months ago        4.94GB
```

Notice that the new Server Core base container image was updated and the previous one now has no tags. Since they have different image IDs, we could remove the previous image – if there are no more containers using it.

The main thing here is that if we run another container based on the new image, we can see the new KBs applied:

```
PS C:\windows\system32> docker run --entrypoint powershell -it mcr.
microsoft.com/windows/servercore:ltsc2019
Windows PowerShell
Copyright (C) Microsoft Corporation. All rights reserved.

PS C:\> systeminfo /fo csv | ConvertFrom-Csv | select OS*, System*,
Hotfix* | Format-List
```

```
OS Name             : Microsoft Windows Server 2019 Datacenter
OS Version          : 10.0.17763 N/A Build 17763
OS Manufacturer     : Microsoft Corporation
OS Configuration    : Standalone Server
OS Build Type       : Multiprocessor Free
System Boot Time    : 6/10/2020, 11:31:53 AM
System Manufacturer : LENOVO
System Model        : 20BTS05T00
System Type         : x64-based PC
System Directory    : C:\Windows\system32
System Locale       : en-us;English (United States)
Hotfix(s)           : 2 Hotfix(s) Installed.,[01]: KB4562562,[02]:
                      KB4561608
```

Notice the same last line from the preceding output. The KBs applied to the new Server Core container image have a higher number than the previous one.

There's an interesting aspect here: for Windows containers, most of your applications will end up using either Server Core, Nano Server, Windows, IIS, or .Net base images as they cover a lot of ground in terms of Windows applications. The IIS and .Net images are based themselves on the Server Core or Nano Server images, so whenever there's an update to the Server Core or Nano Server images, these images are also updated.

The question then is: If you create a new image based on any of the preceding images, how do you keep *your* image updated? The answer to that is simply running the docker build command again, after the base images were updated in your container host. Here's an overview of the process, as shown in Figure 3-7.

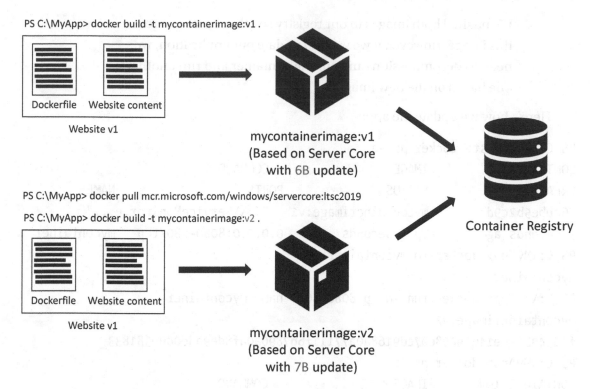

PS C:\MyApp> docker build -t mycontainerimage:v1 .

Dockerfile   Website content

Website v1

mycontainerimage:v1
(Based on Server Core
with 6B update)

PS C:\MyApp> docker pull mcr.microsoft.com/windows/servercore:ltsc2019

PS C:\MyApp> docker build -t mycontainerimage:v2 .

Dockerfile   Website content

Website v1

mycontainerimage:v2
(Based on Server Core
with 7B update)

Container Registry

Figure 3-7. *Updating your container image with new security patches*

Here are a few things to notice on the preceding process:

1. The process to build the container v1 is the same as we showed before. Nothing new here.

2. Once a new security fix is released (Patch Tuesday), you can run the docker pull command for your existing base images.

3. We ran the docker build command again against the same image we created before, but we tagged it v2 so we don't mess with the existing image as we could have containers already running based on this image.

4. Notice we did not change anything in the docker file or the application itself. We simply ran the same docker build command again on the same application folder against the same unaltered docker file.

5. We pushed both images to our registry so other hosts can reuse
   this image. However, if we want to update our application, we
   need to decommission our running container and run another
   one based on the new image.

Here's how we update the app:

```
PS C:\WAC Test> docker ps -a
CONTAINER ID        IMAGE               COMMAND
CREATED             STATUS              PORTS               NAMES
76cbbe5b2c9d        mycontainerimage:v1   "C:\\ServiceMonitor.e..."
5 seconds ago       Up 3 seconds        0.0.0.0:8080->80/tcp   mycontainer
PS C:\MyApp> docker rm mycontainer -f
mycontainer
PS C:\MyApp> docker run -d -p 8080:80 --name mycontainer
mycontainerimage:v2
f4d549b633e14ef9498eb7cd9168a0a77111f6b7890a0af8de9a8d0d9b581833
PS C:\MyApp> docker ps -a
CONTAINER ID        IMAGE               COMMAND
CREATED             STATUS              PORTS               NAMES
76cbbe5b2c9d        mycontainerimage:v2   "C:\\ServiceMonitor.e..."
5 seconds ago       Up 3 seconds        0.0.0.0:8080->80/tcp   mycontainer
```

The first command we used is docker ps to check which containers are running
based on the version 1 of our container image. The second command is the docker rm
which removed the container. We then ran the docker run command to recreate the
container based on the new version 2 of our container image. Next, just to confirm the
new container was running correctly, we ran the docker ps command again. We now
have a new version of our application with the latest security fixes.

Mixing container and container host versions

The topic from the previous section might spark a new conversation all together: What
about containers that have a different version than the container host? The question is:
Should I keep updating and upgrading both container host and container image?

The short answer to that is that whenever possible, you should update both for security updates, and if you have the proper licenses, upgrade the Windows version to leverage new features. However, we all know that's not always possible – either because the Ops team can't validate new patches fast enough, or because the application is not certified for a new release, or because the company doesn't have the necessary license, and so on.

Before we continue, let me pause and just get some terminology straight: For this book, when I refer to update, I mean applying patches that will keep the Windows OS current in relation to Windows Update. When I say upgrade, I mean the process of moving from one version of Windows Server to a newer one – either for the container host or the container.

With this established, another important aspect of Windows Containers is that we have two isolation modes: hypervisor isolation and process isolation, as covered in Chapter 1. As you remember, hypervisor isolation means the container has its own kernel completely isolated from the host. From a container perspective, what that means is if the host is able to spin up the container, the container can pretty much work on its own. However, from a container host perspective, it still needs to be able to recognize the container image. At the end of the day, container hosts will be able to spin up containers based on the same Windows Server version as the host itself or earlier. For example, a Windows Server 2019 container host can spin up a Windows Server 2019 container as well as any previous version of Windows Server all the way back to Windows Server 2016, but it cannot spin up a container with a newer version, such as Windows Server, version 1903, 1909, or 2004. Windows Server, version 2004, container hosts can run hypervisor-isolated containers of its own version and all the way back to Windows Server 2016. The same applies for hypervisor-isolated containers on Windows 10.

For process-isolated containers, this is not true though. Process-isolated containers do share the container host kernel, so in this isolation mode, you can't run different Windows Server versions between container host and container. However, starting with Windows Server 2019 (or Windows Server, version 1809 for that matter), you can run a different updated version of Windows between container host and container. To better understand this, let's take a look at the official nomenclature of Windows. On a Command Prompt window, type the following:

```
C:\windows\system32>ver

Microsoft Windows [Version 10.0.17763.1282]
```

As you can see from the preceding output, there are four parts for the Windows version nomenclature: Major, Minor, Build, and Revision. Since the launch of Windows 10 and Windows Server 2016 (respectively, client and server versions), the Major version has been the same, 10. The Minor version – usually used to differentiate alpha, beta, and released software – hasn't changed from 0 as well. The Build and Revision number will change to reflect new releases of each OS and its updates, respectively. Whenever a new release of Windows 10 or Windows Server is launched, the Build number is updated. When a Windows Update patch is applied, the Revision number is updated.

For process-isolated containers, you can't run different Build versions. If you run Windows Server 2019 on the container host, your images must match that. One caveat here is that Windows Server 2019 was released in both LTSC and SAC. Both releases have a 1809 Build number, so it's OK to run a container host with Windows Server 2019 LTSC and a container with Windows Server, version 1809 SAC. Other than that, if you try to run a container with process isolation with different build, you'll get an error message:

```
PS C:\> docker run -d mcr.microsoft.com/windows/servercore:1803
197ae0ca7ef8d5aeb7c28f4b8502a21a2dc7a3f553b6dd188b9863c29bb03d10
C:\Program Files\Docker\docker.exe: Error response
from daemon: hcsshim::CreateComputeSystem
197ae0ca7ef8d5aeb7c28f4b8502a21a2dc7a3f553b6dd188b9863c29bb03d10: The
container operating system does not match the host operating system.
(extra info: {"SystemType":"Container","Name":"197ae0ca7ef8d5aeb
7c28f4b8502a21a2dc7a3f553b6dd188b9863c29bb03d10","Owner":"docker","Volume
Path":"\\\\?\\Volume{a3f2dac8-705f-4b76-bb58-bc3802163a1a}","IgnoreFlushes
DuringBoot":true,"LayerFolderPath":"C:\\ProgramData\\docker\\windowsfilter
\\197ae0ca7ef8d5aeb7c28f4b8502a21a2dc7a3f553b6dd188b9863c29bb03d10","Layer
s":[{"ID":"f2035d2f-6ea8-5e43-8c5d-328fe197ad87","Path":"C:\\ProgramData\\
docker\\windowsfilter\\aaaf36fbca7ec0083b366858a416801e0db08d08ed426d0cb8a
9630b3456674e"},{"ID":"9e11520b-15e4-5a02-a1e4-1f520386963a","Path":"C:\\
ProgramData\\docker\\windowsfilter\\494979fb21154148e633c3c87f2c2705f89fff1
1910b0e77b47aefcad61719df"}],"HostName":"197ae0ca7ef8","HvPartition":false,
"EndpointList":["96A3CBBA-55DF-400C-B25C-9DBB567A6214"],"AllowUnqualifiedDN
SQuery":true}).
```

The preceding error happened because I tried to run a Windows Server, version 1803, on a Windows Server 2019 host with process isolation. If I run the same command but with hypervisor isolation, that should work:

```
PS C:\> docker run -d --isolation hyperv mcr.microsoft.com/windows/
servercore:1803
7d80c14cf613c95dd3673fee565b3cd18346a09ccc4b2eddc1e835717b505ee0
PS C:\> docker ps -a
CONTAINER ID        IMAGE
COMMAND                     CREATED            STATUS
PORTS                 NAMES
7d80c14cf613        mcr.microsoft.com/windows/servercore:1803
"c:\\windows\\system32..."   8 seconds ago       Exited (0)
3 seconds ago                      inspiring_bartik
```

Notice that the only difference from the previous command is the addition of "--isolation hyperv" parameter. Now that the Build number is clear, let's move to Revision.

The Revision number will change as patches are applied to Windows. For Windows containers, until Windows Server 2019, you had to update the container host and container image at the same time to avoid runtime issues. With Windows Server 2019, you can run a mismatched Revision number between container host and container image. However, you should keep in mind that for security reasons, you should always try to update both with the latest security patches.

A more detailed list of supported scenarios is available here: https://docs.microsoft.com/en-us/virtualization/windowscontainers/deploy-containers/version-compatibility. To recap

1. A container host running hypervisor-isolated containers can run a matching and previous version (Build number) of Windows as the container OS, but no newer versions.

2. A container host running process-isolated containers can run only matching versions (Build number) of Windows as the container OS. However, in this same scenario, the container host or container OS can be updated separately (different Revision numbers).

Best practices in building docker files for Windows Containers

So far, we covered a lot of ground to explain how you can create new container images based on the applications you have running already. Here we wanted to pause and go back to something we covered in Chapter 1. There are two situations on which an application is going to be containerized: at the moment the application is being developed or refactored by a developer or by an IT Pro trying to containerize an existing application that is not maintained by developers anymore.

While I am an IT Pro and infrastructure and operations is at my heart, it would be a disservice for you if I said you can containerize everything by yourself without the help of a developer. If we take just the applications that can be containerized, taking in consideration all the requirements discussed up to here, in some cases, you still might need help in understanding how your application behave so it can be containerized. The reason I'm saying this is because when you open the code of the application on Visual Studio or whatever integrated development environment (IDE) your developer uses, these tools have multiple instrumentations to look at the application and provide a docker file automatically, following all the best practices possible.

With that said, for the cases where you will be containerizing the application yourself, it's important to understand some key aspects that will influence image size, container performance, and so on. This section is focused on well-known cases for Windows container. You should also check the Docker documentation for best practices when authoring a docker file here: `https://docs.docker.com/develop/develop-images/dockerfile_best-practices/`.

Keep dependent commands on the same RUN

Many times when building a new docker file, what I like to do is to build a minimal container with the files I need and run the container interactively so I can test the PowerShell commands and see if they work, instead of putting them in the docker file, running docker build, and trying to debug from there. While this helps me in getting the PowerShell commands straight, I do end up with a bunch of lines of commands, and in some cases, separating them may cause runtime issues. For example, if I need to load the PowerShell snap-in of a PowerShell module to then run a new command, on a docker file, it might look something like

```
RUN powershell Add-PSSnapin WDeploySnapin3.0
RUN powershell Restore-WDPackage -Package .\DockerDemoWebsite.zip
```

The commands, the way they are, will fail on a docker file. The reason they will fail is that every time we start a new command, a new layer is generated. To create new layers, docker builds a new container based on the previous executed layer to then run the new one – on a new container. Well, if the Restore-WDPackage (from Web Deploy) requires that you load the PowerShell snap-in, then this has to be executed in the same PowerShell session, but what you did earlier by separating the lines was to tell docker to run each on a new container. The result is that the snap-in was loaded on a container (which is a layer itself), and then another container with no snap-in loaded tried to run the cmdlet. To avoid this, keep the dependent commands on the same RUN:

```
RUN powershell Add-PSSnapin WDeploySnapin3.0; \
        Restore-WDPackage -Package .\DockerDemoWebsite.zip
```

Notice that the preceding code has only one RUN command. At the end of the first line, we added semicolon ";" which indicates this section of the command is over and backslash "\" to indicate the RUN command will continue at the next line. However, there's a major reason why you should keep commands on the same line.

Running multiple commands on the RUN for improved image size

In addition to the preceding scenario, there's another reason you might want to keep multiple commands on the same RUN. When a new line is created and consequently a new layer, Docker has to load OS components more than once. To avoid loading too many components to your image, you can run multiple commands on the same RUN. Here's what I mean:

```
FROM mcr.microsoft.com/windows/servercore/iis:windowsservercore-ltsc2019
WORKDIR /ViniBeer
COPY . .
RUN PowerShell Install-WindowsFeature NET-Framework-45-ASPNET
RUN PowerShell Install-WindowsFeature Web-Asp-Net45
RUN PowerShell Import-Module WebAdministration; \
        New-WebApplication "ViniBeer" -Site 'Default Web Site'
        -ApplicationPool "DefaultAppPool" -PhysicalPath "C:\ViniBeer"
```

The preceding code is the example I used in the previous chapter in which I was building a new container image for the ViniBeer sample application. What we have in this example is a dedicated RUN line for each PowerShell command. If we analyze the image now, we can see multiple layers were created:

```
PS C:\ViniBeer> docker history vinibeerimage:v1
IMAGE                CREATED              CREATED BY
SIZE                 COMMENT
10eb7bf69100         12 minutes ago       cmd /S /C PowerShell Import-Module
WebAdmini…    5.36MB
e8b878058fb3         12 minutes ago       cmd /S /C PowerShell Install-
WindowsFeature …    160MB
1391dd2ad3d1         13 minutes ago       cmd /S /C PowerShell Install-
WindowsFeature …    173MB
f7fe3e2fcd98         14 minutes ago       cmd /S /C #(nop) COPY
dir:61590cd8c5bb2114ce…    24.7MB
12df307c0da1         14 minutes ago       cmd /S /C #(nop) WORKDIR C:\
ViniBeer             41kB
1dfea62c25d8         2 months ago         cmd /S /C #(nop)  ENTRYPOINT ["C:\\
ServiceMo…    41kB
<missing>            2 months ago         cmd /S /C #(nop)  EXPOSE
80                       41kB
<missing>            2 months ago         cmd /S /C powershell
-Command      Add-Window…    201MB
<missing>            2 months ago         Install update ltsc2019-
amd64                    1.47GB
<missing>            21 months ago        Apply image 1809-RTM-
amd64                    3.47GB
```

The docker history command shows how a specific image was built. It shows you layer by layer what was executed and how much in space each layer is consuming. Here we can see the image we created based on the IIS image has layers from the parent IIS base image and layers based on the preceding docker file. Notice the size of the preceding layers and take a look at the resulting image size:

```
PS C:\ViniBeer> docker images
REPOSITORY                              TAG
IMAGE ID            CREATED             SIZE
vinibeerimage                           v1
10eb7bf69100        16 minutes ago      5.51GB
```

Now, let's change our docker file a little bit:

```
FROM mcr.microsoft.com/windows/servercore/iis:windowsservercore-ltsc2019
WORKDIR /ViniBeer
COPY . .
RUN PowerShell Install-WindowsFeature NET-Framework-45-ASPNET; \
    Install-WindowsFeature Web-Asp-Net45; \
    Import-Module WebAdministration; \
    New-WebApplication "ViniBeer" -Site 'Default Web Site'
    -ApplicationPool "DefaultAppPool" -PhysicalPath "C:\ViniBeer"
```

Now we have all of our PowerShell commands under the same RUN. The one thing to look for here is the semicolon ";" at the end of each command and the backslash "\" for new lines.

Here is the docker history of our image and its final size:

```
PS C:\ViniBeer> docker history vinibeerimage:v2
IMAGE               CREATED             CREATED BY
SIZE                COMMENT
eeba0910cfee        26 seconds ago      cmd /S /C PowerShell Install-
WindowsFeature ...   196MB
d852c633aa94        About a minute ago  cmd /S /C #(nop) COPY
dir:7bddd709e33b80979a...   24.7MB
0cc915a0234b        About a minute ago  cmd /S /C #(nop) WORKDIR C:\
ViniBeer            41kB
0916eec6d2f2        12 days ago         cmd /S /C #(nop)  ENTRYPOINT
["C:\\ServiceMo…    41kB
<missing>           12 days ago         cmd /S /C #(nop)  EXPOSE
80                  41kB
<missing>           12 days ago         cmd /S /C powershell
-Command    Add-Window...   200MB
```

```
<missing>              2 weeks ago                Install update ltsc2019-amd64
1.28GB
<missing>              6 weeks ago                Apply image 1809-RTM-
amd64                       3.7GB
PS C:\ViniBeer> docker images
REPOSITORY                                     TAG
IMAGE ID           CREATED           SIZE
vinibeerimage                                  v2
eeba0910cfee       40 seconds ago    5.4GB
```

As you can see, we have fewer layers on this same image, and the total size of the image is 110MB smaller. If you think that this is just a simple sample application and that you will be pushing and pulling this image, that's a considerable save. The larger and complex the application, the more you can save by keeping everything on the same RUN command.

Avoiding escape issues with PowerShell

The concept of escaping when reading code or a script is when the code or script language interpreter thinks a character indicates that another command is coming or that the command finalized when in fact the character was just part of the command itself.

In the previous example, we used a combination of PowerShell commands and the same RUN. To clean up the docker file, we ran each command in its own line so it's easier to read. On a docker file, there are two ways you can move to the next line on the same command. You can either use the default backslash "\" character, or you can use grave accent "`" character. However, the backslash "\" character is also used to indicate a file or folder patch, such as C:\MyApp. For that reason, you might want to use the grave accent "`" option as it avoids issues in using backslash when passing file and folder paths.

If you decide to use the grave accent "`" character, you should specify that at the beginning of your docker file. Here's the same example as the previous section using the grave accent "`" character:

```
# escape=`
FROM mcr.microsoft.com/windows/servercore/iis:windowsservercore-ltsc2019
WORKDIR /ViniBeer
```

```
COPY . .
RUN PowerShell Install-WindowsFeature NET-Framework-45-ASPNET; `
    Install-WindowsFeature Web-Asp-Net45; `
    Import-Module WebAdministration; `
    New-WebApplication "ViniBeer" -Site 'Default Web Site'
    -ApplicationPool "DefaultAppPool" -PhysicalPath "C:\ViniBeer"
```

At the very first line, we added the instruction for docker build to consider "`" as the cue to continue on the next line. Now, if we needed to use the backslash character anywhere, we should not have problems with this docker file.

Another issue that might happen in terms of escaping inside the docker is when using double quotes such as "C:\My Folder". In this example, we have a folder that has a blank space as part of the folder path. However, for the docker file, double quotes should be used to indicate a value to a parameter with no spaces. If there are spaces, the docker file will escape the double quotes. To avoid that, you can change the double quotes for single quotes, such as 'C:\My Folder'. The very example we just used in the preceding text has a case in which we had to change the double quotes for single quotes for the Default Web Site which contains blank spaces in its name.

Don't load unnecessary files into your image

Still talking about image sizes, one of the things you might want to keep in mind is what you really have to load into your image. For example, let's say your application is currently located on a folder called C:\MyApplication. This folder might contain your application but also a number of other unnecessary files that were used to build the application itself. The very docker file is an example of a file that you don't need to load into the image – although its size is almost negligible.

The point here is that you can use a .dockerignore file in the folder of your application to indicate which files or file types you don't want to load into the image. One example is for temporary files and folders you don't want to load, or any executable that is currently in your application folder but is not necessary for the application to work, or even Visual Studio files from the source, and so many other examples.

The .dockerignore file is a simple file that should be in the root directory along with the dockerfile. When the docker build runs, it will read the COPY and ADD commands from the dockerfile, but ignore the items passed on the .dockerignore file. Here are some examples of what you can add to a .dockerignore file:

```
#Comments are accepted in a .dockerignore file
#Exclude dockerfile and .dockerignore
dockerfile
.dockerignore
#Exclude any file or folder with that starts with temp
*/temp*
#Exclude any Visual Studio project file
*.csproj
```

Another thing to keep in mind are files you have to load into the image but can be removed after the image is built. For example, in previous examples, we used

```
RUN Invoke-WebRequest https://download.microsoft.com/download/0/1/
D/01DC28EA-638C-4A22-A57B-4CEF97755C6C/WebDeploy_amd64_en-US.msi -OutFile
./webdeploy.msi; `
        Start-Process msiexec -Wait -ArgumentList '/I C:\DockerDemo\
        webdeploy.msi /quiet /NoRestart /passive ADDLOCAL=ALL
        LicenseAccepted="0"'; `
        Add-PSSnapin WDeploySnapin3.0; `
        Restore-WDPackage -Package .\DockerDemoWebsite.zip
```

The preceding code will download the Web Deploy executable, install it, and load its PowerShell snap-in to then restore the web application package. However, the Web Deploy installation file will continue to exist in the image, although it is completely unnecessary since the application only needs to be installed once. Another option would be to add the following at the end of the preceding code:

```
        Remove-Item -Path ./webdeploy.msi
```

This will remove the file, and then we can end the image knowing we removed unnecessary used space.

Multi-stage builds

The concept of multi-stage build is a bit more complex to grasp, and I'd recommend you use in cases where you have the instructions on how your application works and what its dependencies are. The idea of multi-stage builds is to further reduce the size of container images by leveraging the docker build cache. Because the docker build caches the layers it used, you can put your commands in an order on which you can copy and install necessary components, to then leverage another image to build your final layer. This reduces the image size drastically. The downside of this method is that you can easily forget to copy an important component that will end up breaking your application.

To demonstrate how to use multi-stage builds, I'll be using a sample from the .Net Framework team for ASP.Net applications available at https://github.com/microsoft/dotnet-framework-docker/blob/master/samples/aspnetapp/Dockerfile:

```
FROM mcr.microsoft.com/dotnet/framework/sdk:4.8 AS build
WORKDIR /app

# copy csproj and restore as distinct layers
COPY *.sln .
COPY aspnetapp/*.csproj ./aspnetapp/
COPY aspnetapp/*.config ./aspnetapp/
RUN nuget restore

# copy everything else and build app
COPY aspnetapp/. ./aspnetapp/
WORKDIR /app/aspnetapp
RUN msbuild /p:Configuration=Release

FROM mcr.microsoft.com/dotnet/framework/aspnet:4.8 AS runtime
WORKDIR /inetpub/wwwroot
COPY --from=build /app/aspnetapp/. ./
```

Starting from the top, you can see the example uses the SDK image from .Net Framework. This is a somewhat large image that has many .Net Framework dependencies. This image was created with multi-stage build in mind. Since the goal is not to use this image as the final base image, it's totally OK that the image has components we'll never use. We only needed to prepare our application.

Next, we see the WORKDIR command which is also not new. Then the example copies many files into the image in order to run the "Nuget restore" command. This command is a regular .Net command used to restore any dependency the developer used to develop this particular application and is not something new to containers.

Next, the example copies additional files and creates a new folder specifically to deploy the application. The msbuild command is the .Net command – again, not exclusive to containers – used to deploy the application itself into the newly created folder.

While this flow has deployed the application correctly, it has left behind many unnecessary components that are not utilized by IIS in the case of ASP.Net applications. So the solution here is to call another FROM command and start with a fresh image, which is what the second FROM in the preceding example does. We then create a new folder to host our application. The preceding final command is what does the trick. It copies the content from the cached layers in the previous commands to the new layer in the new image, bringing only the necessary components to it. This drastically reduces the size of the final image and makes it easier to push and pull between container hosts and registries.

In this chapter, we covered a lot of ground on getting your Windows applications into containers and how to get them running correctly. Now it's time to look at some key infrastructure components that your containers will rely on, such as storage, networking, and many more – that's what we'll cover in Chapter 4.

Managing resources in Windows Containers

We covered a lot of ground so far. If you read through the previous chapters, at this point, you have a good understanding and some experience with Windows Containers. At this point, you know what containers are and the role they play on DevOps and the whole spectrum of tools to support those practices. You also understand the concepts of Windows Containers from its architecture to its differences to Linux containers, use cases for Windows Containers, and much more. We also looked at the implementation of Windows containers from very simple examples to more complex ones and some best practices for deploying containers in general and some that are exclusive to the Windows side of the world.

However, let's be honest. The reason you acquired this book is not to get general concepts or examples on how to deploy or implement Windows Containers, right? It's like buying a car. You go to the dealership and talk to the salesperson on what are the features of the new car, such as horsepower, AWD vs. 4x4, gas per mileage, and all other options available. Then you take the car for a test drive, and that's fine. What you really want though is to take the car out for a ride and that's when you realize a bunch other stuff about it that you could never have thought until you took the car to an open road on your own.

From now on, that's what we pursue in this book. At the end of the day, developers can help you package the application, but you are the IT Pro, and with that, you should be able to not only deploy Windows Container but also ensure business requirements are met, that the container is running with the proper resources, that you can manage and troubleshoot it, and all other administrative tasks that are expected from someone operating the production environment of your company's applications.

© Vinicius Ramos Apolinario 2021
V. Ramos Apolinario, *Windows Containers for IT Pros*, https://doi.org/10.1007/978-1-4842-6686-1_4

In this chapter, we will cover the most basic aspects of managing Windows Containers on a day-to-day basis, such as the following:

- How do I limit the amount of resources a container can use?

- How do I provide persistent storage to Windows Containers so my application can store its data?

- How do I properly connect Windows Containers to my network and other external resources?

While going through this chapter, some of the concepts such as restraining how much memory or CPU a container might get might seem similar to VMs. However, keep in mind the architecture differences between the two technologies. More importantly, remember that containers were created with a different purpose than VMs. It's easy to ask questions that are pertinent to the VMs side of the world, but when it comes to containers, you have to remember the use cases are different.

The first thing to remember is that containers share the same kernel as their host. Because of that, any aspect of resource constraints, such as limiting how much CPU a container should have access to or how much memory it can allocate, is a little bit different than VMs. With VMs, you have mechanisms in place to say what is the hardware that will be dedicated to the VM. Once the VM is on, that hardware is available for that guest partition and kernel. Of course, there are mechanisms to add and remove hardware to and from a VM as needed, but the point is that once the hardware is allocated, it is available for the VM and the guest OS on its entirety. For containers, the process is not exactly like that.

Containers share the same kernel as the container host, so any resource constraint happens in kernel mode. In order to achieve that, the processes started by the containers are allocated as a job object. On Windows, job objects allow management of a group of processes as one single unit. While the concept of job objects is not exclusive to containers, it comes in handy for Windows Containers as we can now apply a limit to a parent job object, and that will be inherited by the child process of the container. For containers with hypervisor isolation, the same principle applies, but the higher level in this case is the utility VM.

One interesting aspect of job objects in Windows is that it is very similar to Control Groups (cgroups) on Linux. cgroups on Linux also serve the purpose of grouping multiple processes for management purposes, and it happens that Docker uses it (just like job objects on Windows) to apply resource constraints to containers.

Finally, the other thing to keep in mind on Windows is that Docker is the layer on which you will be applying the configuration for your containers but is not the only one. Docker has its engine which is in itself a layer as we learned in the previous chapter. However, the Docker engine (also referred as docker daemon) will interact with a Windows layer responsible for operating the container. That layer is called Host Compute Service (HCS). HCS is a fairly new implementation on Windows to make the process of Docker calling low-level APIs in the OS simpler. Although HCS was created primarily for Windows Containers, its usage is not limited to Docker, and in fact, there's an open source project called HCS Shim available so other projects can use the HCS layer. More details on this project are available here: `https://github.com/microsoft/hcsshim`.

For the purpose of this book and to ensure you know how to apply resource constraints to containers, there are a few things I want you to keep in mind: There are multiple ways to implement resource constraints or even add and remove hardware and resources to and from Windows containers. The way we'll look at it from this book for educational purposes is through Docker. However, keep in mind that a container orchestrator such as Kubernetes or even Docker Swarm will have its own way to implement the same logic. At the end of the day, they all have to call the HCS layer on Windows.

With all that said, let's get started.

Managing CPU and memory for Windows Containers

When creating VMs, one of the first things you'll notice on any virtualization platform is the option to specify how much memory and CPU you want to dedicate to that specific VM. Even on the cloud, you pay for the size of the VM based, among other things, on how much CPU and memory that VM has. When transitioning from VMs to containers, it's easy for an IT Pro to ask the same question: How much CPU and memory is this container consuming and what are its limits?

As I mentioned in the previous section and in previous chapters, the use case for containers might be completely different than VMs. For that reason, you should always question if imposing a limit to a container is in the best interest of that application or the environment itself. For example, if you have a container that hosts a web application and runs side by side with other containers also hosting web or other types of applications that are long-lived, you might want to limit how much memory and CPU those containers are allowed to allocate to ensure no container can use all resources available or impact the performance of its neighbors. However, for cases of short-lived processes in which your container is brought up to run a specific functionality and is brought down soon after and/or has no other concurrent workloads, you might want to ensure it has the resources to run its function as fast as possible. These are all considerations that are new to IT Pros transitioning from VMs to containers.

To get started on this, let's look at the most basic scenario. So far, we brought up containers, and we never set what are the limits for these containers. How do we know how much memory and CPU a container is using? The answer to that is a new command we'll be covering in this chapter – the docker inspect.

For the next example, I created a container using the following command:

```
PS C:\> docker run -d -p 8080:80 --name mycontainer vinibeerimage:v2
c7347e8fd7fb238510c47ec2bff8ba5a3f86fb1a46835288d444a8cfdbce6566
```

Nothing new with the preceding command, but notice I did not set a limit for memory or CPU, just like in previous examples. The next command I'll run is the docker inspect:

```
PS C:\> docker inspect mycontainer
```

The docker inspect is a very helpful command and can be used to troubleshoot containers as it contains all the information about the container or image you want to inspect. This command can be used on multiple Docker objects, such as images. Since each object contains a lot of metadata, the output of the preceding command will be exceptionally long and would easily consume around eight pages of this book. My recommendation is that you run the command in your environment and check out its default output, but here we will focus on the CPU and memory configuration.

If you browse through the preceding output, the first thing you'll might notice is that the information is formatted using the JavaScript Object Notation (JSON) which is an open format to structure data in a human-friendly way to read it that can also be used to process information by applications. Docker, Kubernetes, and many other container-related tools and frameworks use the JSON format, so it's nice to start wrapping your head around it.

The JSON format uses a notation on which attributes value pairs to an array. What that means is that when you read a JSON, you'll see something like a block of data that starts with something like "host" and underneath it a bunch of settings and its values. For the preceding example, you have the following block (notice that parts of the settings and values of this block were omitted as the HostConfig block is fairly large):

```
"HostConfig": {
        "Binds": null,
        "ContainerIDFile": "",
        "LogConfig": {
            "Type": "json-file",
            "Config": {}
        },
        "NetworkMode": "default",
        "PortBindings": {
            "80/tcp": [
                {
                    "HostIp": "",
                    "HostPort": "8080"
                }
            ]
        },
        [omitted...]
        "Isolation": "process",
        "CpuShares": 0,
        "Memory": 0,
        "NanoCpus": 0,
        "CgroupParent": "",
        "BlkioWeight": 0,
        "BlkioWeightDevice": [],
        "BlkioDeviceReadBps": null,
        "BlkioDeviceWriteBps": null,
        "BlkioDeviceReadIOps": null,
        "BlkioDeviceWriteIOps": null,
        "CpuPeriod": 0,
        "CpuQuota": 0,
        "CpuRealtimePeriod": 0,
        "CpuRealtimeRuntime": 0,
        "CpusetCpus": "",
        "CpusetMems": "",
        [omitted...]
```

```
        "CpuCount": 0,
        "CpuPercent": 0,
        "IOMaximumIOps": 0,
        "IOMaximumBandwidth": 0,
        "MaskedPaths": null,
        "ReadonlyPaths": null
    },
```

There are multiple configurations in the preceding code that are related to memory and CPU. The ones we're looking for here are "Memory" and "NanoCpus". These values will show us how much memory and CPU this specific container can allocate. To make it easier to get that information, we can filter the data directly in the docker inspect command:

```
PS C:\> docker inspect --format='{{.HostConfig.Memory}}' mycontainer
0
PS C:\> docker inspect --format='{{.HostConfig.NanoCpus}}' mycontainer
0
```

First, let's look at the command itself. The docker inspect command allows you to filter the output by stating what is the information you need from the JSON format it would show by default. In order to do that, you can use the parameter --format. The format option has a standard as you see in the preceding example, such as --format='{{. HostConfig.Memory}}'. The HostConfig is one of the blocks you can pass on the --format option, and to know which option to show, you would have to run the full output once and check for the information you're looking for.

In the case of the preceding example, we are looking for the memory and CPU limit for this container, which is represented in the settings "Memory" and "NanoCpus" under the HostConfig block. You'll notice the value for these settings is returning 0. That's because the container has no enforced limit on how much memory and CPU it can have allocated.

The interesting thing here is that this output shows the enforced (or not) configuration of the container, but not the real-time utilization. If you'd like to check the allocated resources to a container (or all containers), you can use another command – docker stats:

```
PS C:\> docker stats --no-stream
CONTAINER ID   NAME           CPU %   sssPRIV WORKING SET   NET I/O          BLOCK I/O
a6c78a71c5f6   mycontainer3   0.00%   56.77MiB              106B / 2.94kB    12.2MB / 1.35MB
a08e76b847bc   mycontainer2   1.10%   57.7MiB               14.4kB / 12.3kB  12.3MB / 1.47MB
ff0ec61e8f28   mycontainer1   0.00%   58.23MiB              16.9kB / 12.1kB  21.1MB / 1.55MB
c7347e8fd7fb   mycontainer    0.00%   58.55MiB              2.12MB / 878kB   180MB / 40MB
```

The docker stats command is very simple and returns the stats for the running
containers. It works pretty much as the performance tab on Task Manager or
Performance Monitor. By default, if you run just docker stats, the command will clean
the PowerShell window and keep a refreshed view of the allocated resources to a
container. If you just want to check the allocated resources on that specific moment, you
can run the docker stats command with the --no-stream option. Also, by default, the
docker stats command will only show the running containers. If you want to show the
stats for all containers – including the ones that are stopped – you can add the -a option,
although that's not very helpful as you can see in the following in which mycontainer1 is
stopped, so the allocation of everything returns 0:

```
PS C:\> docker stats -a --no-stream
CONTAINER ID   NAME           CPU %   PRIV WORKING SET   NET I/O          BLOCK I/O
a6c78a71c5f6   mycontainer3   0.00%   65.51MiB           418kB / 271kB    19.9MB / 16.6MB
a08e76b847bc   mycontainer2   1.15%   65.7MiB            432kB / 270kB    20.3MB / 16.5MB
ff0ec61e8f28   mycontainer1   0.00%   0B                 0B / 0B          0B / 0B
c7347e8fd7fb   mycontainer    0.00%   58.62MiB           2.12MB / 881kB   180MB / 40MB
```

Before we go back to our goal for this section, which is to limit how much memory
and CPU a container can allocate, the final item to keep in mind is how much we can
define in the container configuration. We need to know the Docker settings for this host
so we can allocate the appropriate amount of hardware resources. To check on that, you
can use the docker info command:

```
PS C:\> docker info
Client:
 Debug Mode: false
 Plugins:
  cluster: Manage Docker clusters (Docker Inc., v1.2.0)
```

```
Server:
 Containers: 4
  Running: 3
  Paused: 0
  Stopped: 1
 Images: 20
 Server Version: 19.03.3
 Storage Driver: windowsfilter
  Windows:
 Logging Driver: json-file
 Plugins:
  Volume: local
  Network: ics internal l2bridge l2tunnel nat null overlay private
  transparent
  Log: awslogs etwlogs fluentd gcplogs gelf json-file local logentries
  splunk syslog
 Swarm: inactive
 Default Isolation: process
 Kernel Version: 10.0 17763 (17763.1.amd64fre.rs5_release.180914-1434)
 Operating System: Windows Server 2019 Datacenter Version 1809 (OS Build
 17763.1282)
 OSType: windows
 Architecture: x86_64
 CPUs: 4
 Total Memory: 7.688GiB
 Name: VINIAP-2019HOST
 ID: YOWC:G7UB:TKLB:ENXI:55TN:MGPA:KTZJ:QUXR:2VSK:D224:IXJB:ZT6V
 Docker Root Dir: C:\ProgramData\docker
 Debug Mode: false
 Registry: https://index.docker.io/v1/
 Labels:
 Experimental: false
 Insecure Registries:
  127.0.0.0/8
 Live Restore Enabled: false
```

For the information we're after, we can use the preceding command to check the CPUs and Total Memory. As you can see, for the container host I'm using, I can allocate a total of 4 CPUs and I have 7.688GiB – keep in mind that just like with VMs, you can't allocate all that memory to a container as the host has its own processes as well.

As we observed earlier, the JSON output of the inspection on the container returns the value we're looking for. In order to change that configuration, we can set the parameter for the container when we first create it with docker run:

```
PS C:\> docker run -d -p 8084:80 --cpus=1 --name mycontainer4 vinibeerimage:v2
dbbf6e6b0f713d1c0615e0a619ae9cf5ac6246043af5993a6df228ad60bfbe21
```

Notice that the only change to the usual docker run command that we saw up until now is the addition of --cpus=1. This will inform Docker that this container cannot allocate more than one CPU. Here, let me pause for a second and explain how this allocation occurs. Just like VMs, containers will allocate CPU cycles that can be a percentage of a CPU power, the totality of a CPU, or even more than one CPU. Setting the configuration of --cpus to 1 means we're giving this container the ability to allocate 100% of one CPU. The container will not be able to allocate more than one CPU, and if that's required, you may observe a performance degradation for the application running on that container – although that's the expected result, which is the opposite of this container taking all cycles from other containers.

The reason I'm explaining that is because you also have the option to set up 1.5 to --cpus. Setting up 1.5 means the container can use 100% of one CPU and 50% of a second CPU. In fact, you could even configure a minimum of .1. That means 10% of one CPU, but keep in mind that this would severely impact the overall performance of the container and its application.

To check on the result of the preceding configuration, let's use the same command we used before:

```
PS C:\> docker inspect --format='{{.HostConfig.NanoCpus}}' mycontainer4
1000000000
```

The result of the configuration is shown in the output; however, it's a bit confusing. The value returned is not exactly a percentage, but the calculation of CPU period * CPU quota. These values are settings available for the Docker on Linux, and in those scenarios, you could set up these values to get an even granular configuration. Although these settings are not available for Docker on Windows, the way CPUs are calculated still relies on these other settings. Let's look at another option:

```
PS C:\> docker run -d -p 8085:80 --cpus=1.5 --name mycontainer5
vinibeerimage:v2
9341b7f9c90cf1236cc4f784ee9a5e88cc83ca1bf995be16bfbae75955018195
PS C:\> docker run -d -p 8086:80 --cpus=.5 --name mycontainer6
vinibeerimage:v2
94129381db50c081ef55e1ce42ea83209046bdd8742de353e2c8a3f78d86d643
PS C:\> docker run -d -p 8087:80 --cpus=3 --name mycontainer7
vinibeerimage:v2
df6103a63c459c2c400acef20f91eab980632e03010365299de3918319c3df92
PS C:\> docker inspect --format='{{.HostConfig.NanoCpus}}' mycontainer5
1500000000
PS C:\> docker inspect --format='{{.HostConfig.NanoCpus}}' mycontainer6
500000000
PS C:\> docker inspect --format='{{.HostConfig.NanoCpus}}' mycontainer7
3000000000
```

In the preceding examples, I created three new containers with different CPU configuration. Then I used the docker inspect to show the value associated to how much CPU these containers can allocate. Now let's look at the memory configuration.

Just like CPU, we can set up the memory configuration at the moment we create the container using docker run:

```
PS C:\> docker run -d -p 8087:80 -m 2048 --name mycontainer
vinibeerimage:v2
f305f44ec71dcffdc1a915119450e73c698adf6caa08798362f4a891ebf9d437
```

Just like the CPU option, the only item we added here is the -m setting. This option can be used in different formats, and that would affect the granularity of how much memory the container can allocate. You can either use megabytes by representing it with "2048" for 2048 megabytes, or you can use 2Gb to say this container can allocate

2 gigabytes. However, this representation does take in consideration the calculation of megabytes vs. gigabytes. Up until the writing of this book, Docker does not consider GiB which is a new standard used to fix the issue of calculating Mb vs. Gb. Here's what I mean:

```
PS C:\> docker run -d -p 8080:80 -m 2048 --name mycontainer
vinibeerimage:v2
731afcabb2f35f6d33c6876765bbd8de1e6d76e8d7e58f08429a0e216d169560
PS C:\> docker run -d -p 8081:80 -m 2Gb --name mycontainer1
vinibeerimage:v2
6181eeea68c6ea7e9660a07581036bdd48452b3099f84a7ac957e08ff59a1e2b
```

Theoretically, the preceding two commands are setting a limit to the container of 2Gb of memory. However, look at the output of docker inspect:

```
PS C:\> docker inspect --format='{{.HostConfig.Memory}}' mycontainer
2048
PS C:\> docker inspect --format='{{.HostConfig.Memory}}' mycontainer1
2147483648
```

The first container was created with -m 2048 and the second one with -m 2Gb. The end result is that the first one can allocate 2048 megabytes which translate to 2.0480E+9. The second one can allocate slightly more than that. Realistically, it won't make a difference, but just something to keep in mind. Ideally, you should choose one option and go with that for all containers you create, just to avoid any confusion.

Just like CPU, the configuration of memory for Docker on Windows is limited to this option. However, if you look at Docker's documentation or even the help information for the docker run command, you'll notice that there are other parameters available for Docker on Linux. As of the writing of this book, both CPU and memory are limited to these two commands for specifying absolute numbers on which the container will have that specific limit for that given item.

Storage overview for containers

As an IT Pro, you are probably familiar with many storage-related concepts, mostly probably tied to file system types such as NTFS or ReFS, connection types such as iSCSI or Fiber Channel, protocols such as Server Message Block (SMB) or Network File System

(NFS), and so on. For containers, we already covered another concept called scratch space. To recap, scratch space means that when a container is on, all of its writing operations happen in a scratch space that is not persisted when a new instance of that container is created. It's important to keep in mind that if you start a container, write something on its C:\ drive, stop the container, and start it again, you'll still see the data. However, because of the nature of containers, we learned that we cannot expect that the same instance of a container will be started. For microservices environments, it's expected that a container will run for the period on which the application is executing something and threw away once its processing is completed.

For scenarios in which we lift and shift an application from a VM or bare metal to a container, that given application might not be aware of this behavior, so it's your job to ensure the application stores the data in a persistent storage.

In some cases, though, you might not even need a persistent storage. Let's look at the example of a web server running an instance of IIS that connects to a SQL Server instance. Most of the time, the SQL Server instance is running on another server, so originally you have VM instances of your web application connecting to a back-end SQL Server database on another VM. If you move the IIS instances to a container, they will still try to connect to the same SQL Server database. What you need to ensure is that the container instances have networking access to the SQL Server database. In these cases, what you need to ensure is that the container itself has enough storage to host the web application (or any other application type for that matter) so it can run correctly. Let's start by looking at the default storage configuration of Windows Containers.

First, remember from Chapter 1 that all containers are created from a container image and that each container image is composed of multiple layers. When a new writing operation is executed, the data is stored on the scratch space. However, the container OS still sees the C:\ drive as a storage location just like any other Windows deployment. By default, the container will see a C:\ drive with a total of 20GB. If you start a new container and open an interactive session to it, you can check that as the following example:

```
PS C:\> docker run --entrypoint powershell -it --name testcontainer mcr.
microsoft.com/windows/servercore:ltsc2019
PS C:\> Get-WmiObject win32_logicaldisk

DeviceID    : C:
DriveType   : 3
```

```
ProviderName :
FreeSpace    : 21181349888
Size         : 21339549696
VolumeName   :
```

In some cases, the application you want to run on a Windows Container might require more space. You can change that behavior when creating a new container by using the option --storage-opt when creating the container with docker run. Here's an example:

```
PS C:\> docker run -d -p 8080:80 --storage-opt "size=50GB" --name
mycontainer vinibeerimage:v2
52694412030b1244cad3c511b81608b2207d3b5fe0c42b542ab15d0b6d142c9f
```

In the preceding example, we set up a C:\ drive with 50GB of total available storage. If you run the same preceding command to check on the disk space, here's what you get:

```
PS C:\> Get-WmiObject win32_logicaldisk

DeviceID     : C:
DriveType    : 3
ProviderName :
FreeSpace    : 53395660800
Size         : 53551800320
VolumeName   :
```

By default, the data stored on the container's native drive – C:\ drive – will be stored on the C:\Program Data\Docker folder on the host. Inside that folder, the data will be split between the image and windowsfilter directories. Notice that when you create a new container, the total allocation of the drive is not allocated on the container host – rather, new data is added when new layers are added. This is a similar behavior from dynamically expanding VHD files, but with the difference that everything is written on layers, which are a different standard than VHD files that just grow in size.

Now that you know how to provide more local storage to a container, you might be interested in changing the default location of where the data for the C:\ drive of your containers is stored on your container host. That is possible by changing a JSON file on the container host that Docker uses to read its configurations. Keep in mind that changing this will affect both layers and scratch space for your containers.

Note   After applying the following configuration, you will have to restart the docker service. Once the service is started, it will read from the new location, but the data won't be transferred. All images, layers, containers, and other data will not be visible. To revert the process, you can remove the file and restart the service again. This change in the configuration is recommended to be executed on a brand-new container host before you start pulling images and creating new containers.

The configuration file that Docker uses to read its configurations can be created at C:\ProgramData\Docker\config\daemon.json. By default, the file won't exist, and Docker will use its default configuration. To change the default location, create the preceding file and write the following on it:

```
{
    "data-root": "d:\\docker"
}
```

The preceding example will use the D:\ drive as the destination and create a folder structure under the docker folder. Here is the end result as shown in Figure 4-1.

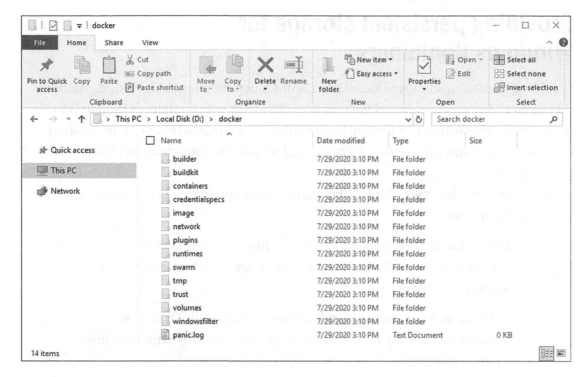

Figure 4-1. *Docker set up to use D:\ drive*

From now on, all Dockers will use the folder on the D:\ drive to store new images and container's layers and scratch spaces.

Note that the daemon.json file can be used for many other configurations as described in the documentation here: `https://docs.microsoft.com/en-us/virtualization/windowscontainers/manage-docker/configure-docker-daemon`.

Setting up the right location for Docker to store the data for native drive of the containers you want to create is an important process and the first step you should take to ensure you are using the correct volumes on your container host. For scenarios on which you have a stateless application, it's fine to simply use the local drive inside the container to store the application itself and ensure appropriate storing on container host. All application data would go somewhere else, such as a remote SQL Server database server which can be a VM or even another container. However, in many other cases, the application is not aware of the nature of container storage, and you need to provide a persistent storage. We'll look into that in the next section.

Providing persistent storage for Windows Containers

Providing persistent storage to a container is not much different than existing methods that as an IT Pro you are already familiar with. The trick with containers though is to understand what is the scenario you have in place – in terms of how your application accesses the data on the persistent storage and what is the configuration you have for your storage.

To get started, let's take a look at the alternatives to providing persistent storage to Windows Containers:

- Bind mounts: The simplest way to provide persistent storage, bind mounts are simply folders on your container host that you can mount inside the container.

- SMB mounts: A variant of bind mounts available after Windows Server, version 1709, allows you to map a network drive from the host to the container.

- Named volumes: This option uses a Docker driver to mount a volume using the Docker engine that makes it available for multiple containers.

Let's explore each option and its implementation.

Bind mounts

This is probably the easiest model for providing persistent storage to Windows Containers. With bind mounts, you can simply specify a folder on your container host that can be mapped inside the container. The advantage of this option is that it is really simple to configure – all you have to do is to specify the -v option when running docker run to create your containers. The downside of bind mounts is that they only work locally for containers running on that container host. In addition to that, while the folder can be accessed by multiple containers at the same time, these containers cannot access the same file at the same time. This is something you are probably familiar with if you ever managed access to a NTFS drive that is shared by multiple servers. Still, bind mounts are very useful. Here's how they work.

In the example we'll go over, we have a container host with a folder called "C:\ MyApp". We will bind mount this folder on a container and explore its usage. Here's a view of the folder from the container host, as shown in Figure 4-2.

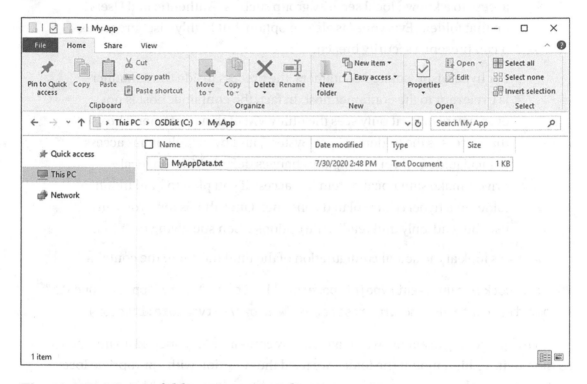

Figure 4-2. *My App folder on container host*

Before we create a new container with a bind mount to this folder, we need to look at the permission used by the container to access this folder – since the folder is sitting on an NTFS drive and will not let an unknown process or user access its data.

The key here is to identify which isolation mode you'll be using to run the container. You can bind mount a folder to both hypervisor- and process-isolated containers, but the process and how the authentication happens are a bit different:

- For process-isolated containers, the Access Control List (ACL) on the NTFS drive is honored as the containers are using a process that is known to the container host. Whatever user being used by the container will be passed on to the container host. For well-defined applications using Windows Authentication, this shouldn't be a problem, but if the process inside the container trying to access the folder is using the default user, then that user is not known by the container host. By default, Server Core–based images use the local user called "ContainerAdministrator" and Nano Server–based images use "ContainerUser". In order to solve this, you'd need to provide access to a known local security group such as "Authenticated Users" on that folder. "Everyone" is also an option, but highly discouraged as it can present a security breach.

– For hypervisor-isolated containers, the process inside the container is irrelevant to the container host. In fact, the container host is not even aware of it – it only sees the utility VM of that container. The user that accesses the folder is "LocalSystem", and by default, it has access to local folders. If your company changes default ACLs on local drives, make sure LocalSystem has access if you plan to bind mount a folder in a hypervisor-isolated container. Once that is met, you can use the read-only and read-write options when specifying the mount.

Now let's look at the actual configuration of the bind mount to the container:

```
PS C:\> docker run --entrypoint powershell -it -v "c:\My App:c:\appdata"
--name testcontainer mcr.microsoft.com/windows/servercore:ltsc2019
```

In the preceding example, we created a new container and opened an interactive session to it. To bind mount the folder, we used the -v option with appropriate local folder (from the host) and how the container would see it mapped. The standard for that is to provide the two paths separated by colon ":". It's unfortunate that colon is also used to specify the path, so it's a bit hard to read sometimes. For the preceding example, I used the local path "C:\My App" and the path in the container "c:\appdata". Here are a few things to notice: First, I had to use double quotes for the whole value of the -v parameter as there's a space on the folder path. Also, the path on the container is all lowercase.

Once the session inside the container is open, here's what we see:

```
PS C:\> cd .\appdata\
PS C:\appdata> dir


    Directory: C:\appdata

Mode                LastWriteTime         Length Name
----                -------------         ------ ----
-a----        7/30/2020     2:48 PM           11 MyAppData.txt
```
118

Just like on the container host, we can see the same folder structure and file. We can now create new files in this folder from inside the container – this is because we did not set up which level of permission we'd be setting up for the container, so the default is read-write:

```
PS C:\appdata> New-Item -ItemType File -Name MyAppData1.txt

    Directory: C:\appdata

Mode                 LastWriteTime         Length Name
----                 -------------         ------ ----
-a----        7/30/2020   3:22 PM              0 MyAppData1.txt

PS C:\appdata> dir

    Directory: C:\appdata

Mode                 LastWriteTime         Length Name
----                 -------------         ------ ----
-a----        7/30/2020   2:48 PM             11 MyAppData.txt
-a----        7/30/2020   3:22 PM              0 MyAppData1.txt
```

Since the permission here is read-write, the file is now available on the container host as well. However, different than what you'd might expect, if the permission was read-only, there would be no error message on the container. Rather, the change would be staged in a container layer and would be available for the container only. As expected, that layer would be lost when the container is gone as it would be part of that container's scratch space.

For hypervisor isolation, the process is very similar with the only difference being that you should specify which level of permission you want to use:

```
PS C:\> docker run --entrypoint powershell -it -v c:\MyApp:c:\appdata:RO
--isolation hypcrv --name testcontainer mcr.microsoft.com/windows/
servercore:ltsc2019
```

Notice the :RO after the value of the -v parameter. This indicates read-only. For read-write, you can use :RW. If nothing is provided, the default behavior is read-write.

SMB mount

The bind mount option is very useful for testing and development scenarios. As explained earlier, though, it does present some challenges for production environments on which multi-access to the same file is needed and/or access from multiple container hosts. For that, we can use SMB mounts. SMB mounts should be very familiar to you – this is just a network share (on Windows or a supported SMB share) that you can present to the container host and then map to the containers running on those nodes. In addition to addressing the preceding issues of multi-access to the same file and having the share available to any container host that has access to it, this option also comes with the other benefits of SMB:

- Support for Scale-Out File Server (SOFS) on Storage Spaces Direct (S2D): SOFS is a fairly new feature on Windows Server cluster to support multi-node file servers with high availability. The combination of that with S2D allows you to build your highly available file server using local disks on your cluster nodes, although traditional SAN is also supported. For Windows Containers, this means a very lean infrastructure on which your container hosts also provide a highly available file system that is shared among container hosts and mapped to the containers.

- Cloud-based SMB share: If your container hosts are running in the cloud and you don't want the headache of building a highly available file system that is then mapped to the containers, you can use the services provided by your cloud vendor. Most vendors provide network shares as a service for VMs running on their clouds. One example is Azure Files.

- Traditional file services or network-attached storage (NAS): If you don't need high availability for your SMB share or you want a plug-and-play solution, you can simply build a file server running Windows Server or get an out-of-the-box NAS solution. As long as the network share supports SMB, you should be able to connect to it from the container host and map that share to the containers.

There's one thing to remember before choosing the option of SMB mount: this was introduced on Windows Server, version 1907. If you have a container host running Windows Server 2016, this option is not available.

From the container side, mapping an SMB mount is pretty much the same as a bind mount. There is an additional step to be performed on the container host, though:

```
PS C:\> $creds = Get-Credential
PS C:\> New-SmbGlobalMapping -RemotePath \\myserver\appdata -Credential
$creds -LocalPath E:
```

The preceding commands will prepare the container host with the network share you want to provide to the containers. The first command is native PowerShell cmdlet that will store the credential you provide at the $cred variable. Next, the New-SMBGlobalMapping cmdlet allows you to connect to an SMB share and make that available for other sessions in that machine. All you have to do is provide the path, credential, and local path.

Now let's look at the container side: let's say the path we just mounted on the container host at the E:\ drive has a folder called E:\App1Data. In that case, you can now mount the share just like you did with bind mounts:

```
PS C:\> docker run --entrypoint powershell -it -v e:\App1Data:c:\appdata --
name testcontainer mcr.microsoft.com/windows/servercore:ltsc2019
```

See that the preceding command is the same as used before, with the different path to map the E:\ drive. Different from the bind mount, though, now all users inside the container will have the same access level as the credential you used for mapping the drive.

Named volumes

The two preceding options, bind mount and SMB mount, are kind of native to the OS, and what Docker does is simply pass the file system to the container. The next option we will explore is named volumes, which actually passes to the Docker layer the ownership of dealing on how the containers will write to the persistent storage. According to Docker, there are many advantages of named volumes over bind mounts (and SMB mounts). Mostly the reasons to use this option would be to have a central place to deal with both the containers and its volumes – single place to backup data, manage volumes via Docker CLI, map volumes by name instead of path, and so on. Most importantly, there is an option to have third-party plugins that use the Docker named volumes API to provide additional resources and features. One example is the Azure File Storage plugin that allows you to use Azure Storage as the back end of your named volume, so containers writing to this location would directly connect to an Azure Storage – totally transparent to the container. You can find a list of available plugins here: `https://docs.docker.com/engine/extend/legacy_plugins/`. However, most of these plugins are Linux only. In fact, for on-premises use, the only generic plugin available as of the writing of this book is the native Docker plugin. In any case, we will cover how to use named volumes, so you know how this feature works.

First, we need to create a new volume:

```
PS C:\> docker volume create myvolume
myvolume
```

The preceding command will create a new volume using the default driver (or plugin, as mentioned earlier) and the native storage configurations. If we were using a third-party plugin, we could add the -d option (d is for driver). Installing the plugin following the vendor's instructions would be necessary before using it with the docker volume create command.

We can check the details of the newly created volume:

```
PS C:\> docker volume inspect myvolume
[
    {
        "CreatedAt": "2020-08-02T19:34:05-07:00",
        "Driver": "local",
        "Labels": {},
        "Mountpoint": "C:\\ProgramData\\docker\\volumes\\myvolume\\_data",
        "Name": "myvolume",
        "Options": {},
        "Scope": "local"
    }
]
```

As you can see, the volume was created using the local drive, and the mount point is the same folder used for all persistent storage. Now we can map the volume using only its name:

```
PS C:\> docker run --entrypoint powershell -it -v myvolume:c:\appdata --
name testcontainer mcr.microsoft.com/windows/servercore:ltsc2019
```

Just like the other mount types, all data written from containers into this location will be available to other containers as well. You can write some data into this location, then fire up a new container, and see the information there.

As you can tell by now, each option shown in this section of the chapter has its pros and cons. My recommendation to you is if you are running a dev/test environment, using bind mount is the simplest way to provide persistent storage to a container for testing purposes. When you containerize a legacy application, using SMB mount would probably be the safest option to avoid issues with permissions and easier way to provide high availability. If your company has a storage vendor that provides a Docker volume plugin, make sure you know its benefits and follow its guidance on how to use that plugin.

Networking overview for containers

The final topic of this chapter is also somewhat more complex – just like with physical or virtual machines. Connecting multiple endpoints can be a daunting task if not carefully planned. With containers, this is elevated as microservices environments tend to have short-lived instances and traditional networking devices tend to have trouble associating Internet Protocols (IPs) and Media Access Control (MAC) addresses to short-lived instances. Plus, there are way too many components in play to make the physical and virtual networks work properly. In this section, we will cover some important networking concepts that you need to know and understand in order to properly deploy the networking configuration for your environment. However, we assume you are familiar with some other components and terms, such as Dynamic Host Configuration Protocol (DHCP) server, Domain Name System (DNS), Transmission Control Protocol (TCP) and the Internet Protocol (IP), and some other basic networking concepts, such as Classless Inter-Domain Routing (CIDR). At the end of the day, there are way too many ways you can configure your network, and most probably what you end up having to do is to mimic your already established networking configuration to your container environment.

With all that said, I'd like to start with an analogy to VMs – which I assume is something you are familiar with.

Just like VMs, containers share a networking connection with the host. Of course, there are test/dev scenarios in which you can create a private or internal virtual switch and the VMs can connect to themselves and the host only, but even in these cases, the VMs have a virtual network interface card (NIC) and that NIC is connected to the physical NIC on the host via a virtual switch. For containers, the process is pretty much the same, with some differences in terminologies and components. If we were to put a VM and a container side by side on a VM and container host, they would look remarkably similar from a networking standpoint, as you can see on Figure 4-3.

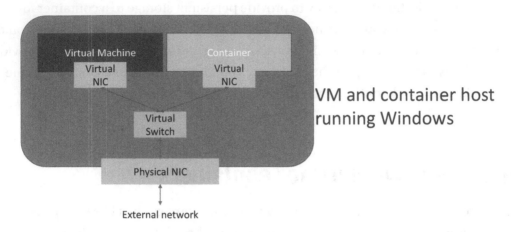

Figure 4-3. *VM and container virtual NIC*

The differences of VM and container from a networking standpoint start on the virtual switch that each uses. On a Hyper-V host, you can manage the virtual switches via PowerShell or Hyper-V Manager (or any other management platform, such as System Center, Windows Admin Center, etc.). External switches created for Hyper-V VMs can be reused for containers. Let's take a look at how we check virtual switches for our containers:

```
PS C:\> docker network ls
NETWORK ID          NAME                DRIVER              SCOPE
9d3c7a5fcc99        External Network    transparent         local
49ad25853dcb        nat                 nat                 local
91a6ec72874c        none                null                local
```

The command docker network is the command to manage all networking-related configuration for containers. The ls option lists the networks available for your containers. Notice that in the preceding example, three networks are available for my containers on my container host, but I never created a new network via Docker – this was all there by default. You will also notice the preceding DRIVER column on which we can see what type of network each entry is using.

The "nat" network is the default one and is created when Docker is installed on a container host. You saw this network in previous chapters, and we already used it to map a port from the container host to a port on the container, allowing us to access an application running inside the container. However, there are more options for networking configurations. Let's look at each one:

- NAT: This option is equivalent to an "Internal" virtual switch type on Hyper-V. The Network Address Translation (NAT) is a well-established concept in IT and means that an IP address will be used as destination by a client and the server side will take care of translating the access to the endpoint behind it. For containers, this means you can access the IP address of the host that can be translated to the IP address of the container – port by port. From a virtual switch standpoint, what this means is that all containers connected to this NAT network will have a private IP that has a scope for this specific NAT network, and for all external communication, the IP and MAC address of the host will be used. This option is ideal for scenarios on which you want to validate if an app works correctly on a container, but very challenging on production environments as you'd have to keep track of all translations.

- Transparent: This option is equivalent to an "External" virtual switch type on Hyper-V. Containers connected to this network will have a "transparent" access to the external network via an external virtual switch. You can let the containers request an IP address from your DHCP server, or you can set up a subnet for this network directly via Docker. Just like when you use a nested virtualization scenario (on which you have a VM on top of another VM), if you use this option on a virtualized container host, you'll have to enable MAC address spoofing, which makes this option not suitable for cloud scenarios. For small environments or scenarios on which you have long-lived containers, this might be a fine solution. However, if you have a large deployment and short-lived containers, this might stress your physical switch as it would have to learn an absurd amount of MAC address from all containers that are popping up.

The preceding two options are the simplest ones and the ones we'll be looking at in this book. However, there are additional networking options for when you have even larger environments that are dependent on your choice of container orchestrator. Let's take a look at what they are and when to use:

- Overlay: This is the preferred option for Docker Swarm. It is very similar to virtual switches in VM virtual networks – it allows containers on multiple nodes to use the same virtual network using Virtual Extensible LAN (VXLAN), a protocol created by VMware, CISCO, and other companies. Overlay can also be used by other container orchestrators, such as Kubernetes, but it requires a third-party plugin, such as Flannel, making this a nontrivial option for anything outside Docker Swarm.

- L2bridge: This option is very similar to the preceding transparent option. That means the containers will be connected to an "External" virtual switch, but in the case of l2bridge, a layer-2 MAC-rewrite happens for all containers, so their ingress and egress packets keep the host MAC address. This helps in situations as mentioned earlier in which a physical switch might be overwhelmed by short-lived containers. This is the most common option for Windows scenarios using Kubernetes and can be configured to either use the IP subnet you already have established with a DHCP server or to use a dedicated subnet.

- L2tunnel: This option is the same as l2bridge, but for use on Azure-based infrastructures, such as Microsoft Azure or Azure Stack Hub. Let's say you decide to run container hosts that are Azure VMs and use Kubernetes as your container orchestrator. In that case, you should use this option as it would know how to communicate with the underlying software-defined network configuration in Azure.

Finally, the other piece of this puzzle is how Docker talks to the Windows layer to make all of this work. As mentioned previously, all the compute operations under the Docker layer are processed by a component on Windows called Host Compute Service (HCS). For all networking pieces, another component on Windows is used: Host Networking Services (HNS). HNS is responsible for all operations such as creating the appropriate virtual switch depending on the network type; making sure all rules are in place, such as port forwarding and Windows Firewall for NAT; enforcing other rules for non-NAT, such as ACLs; encapsulation; and so on. At the end of the day, regardless if you use just Docker, or Docker Swarm, or Kubernetes (or any other orchestrator), they all call the HNS layer to apply the Windows configurations. For some of these configurations, HNS is not totally on par to Linux features available for Docker. Since the list of non-supported scenarios is always changing with new releases of Windows Server, you should check this page of an updated view: https://docs. microsoft.com/en-us/virtualization/windowscontainers/container-networking/ architecture#unsupported-features-and-network-options.

With that, let's look at the implementation of NAT and transparent networks in action.

Providing different networking options for Windows Containers

Let's get started by looking at the native NAT network provided by Docker. Since this network is created by default, we can use the docker network inspect to look at its details:

```
PS C:\> docker network inspect nat
[
    {
        "Name": "nat",
        "Id": "49ad25853dcb3b3284e763fe7a197906180e04b9b4899134383c
        21a9b4fb32c2",
        "Created": "2020-08-03T12:27:05.0724375-07:00",
        "Scope": "local",
        "Driver": "nat",
        "EnableIPv6": false,
        "IPAM": {
            "Driver": "windows",
            "Options": null,
            "Config": [
                {
                    "Subnet": "172.25.224.0/20",
                    "Gateway": "172.25.224.1"
                }
```

```
            ]
        },
        "Internal": false,
        "Attachable": false,
        "Ingress": false,
        "ConfigFrom": {
            "Network": ""
        },
        "ConfigOnly": false,
        "Containers": {},
        "Options": {
            "com.docker.network.windowsshim.hnsid": "2E647BFC-E623-4808-
            B4B4-92C15C4D03BE",
            "com.docker.network.windowsshim.networkname": "nat"
        },
        "Labels": {}
    }
]
```

From the output of the preceding command, we can see all the details of the default
NAT network. In addition to the details that you would expect, such as its local scope,
and nat driver, we can see some important details like its IP Address Management
(IPAM) with subnet and gateway. Since this is a NAT network, all containers assigned to
this network will get a private IP address from this subnet IP range and will connect to
this virtual gateway. Also, we can see under the options' block of this JSON output the
corresponding HNS data that Docker is using: HNS ID and network name.

Now let's look at how to create a new NAT network and configure its options
manually:

```
PS C:\> docker network create --driver nat --subnet 192.168.0.0/24
--gateway 192.168.0.1 mynatnetwork
e92114a6fbf3b477ad0dcbae4e0494c8a2c23cf188b0ec6eaea50a0befb9bac4
```

The command "docker network create" can be used to create a new network. In
theory, there's only one required argument: the network name. However, that command
will look for a bridge driver type, which is available on Linux. For Windows then,

you need to specify which driver type you want to use and the network name. In the preceding example, I also provided the subnet IP range to be used by the containers and the gateway to be used in this network. You can run the same "docker network ls" and "docker network inspect mynatnetwork" to list the networks available and inspect the newly created network, respectively.

Now that we have the network created, we can create a new container and assign this network to it:

```
PS C:\> docker run -d --network mynatnetwork -p 8080:80 --name
mynatcontainer vinibeerimage:v2
bfa7dc082d8a120668a286bb7ef50c41518455357f98c698b1585ae1369d4d79
PS C:\> docker inspect --format='{{range .NetworkSettings.Networks}}
{{.IPAddress}}{{end}}' mynatcontainer
192.168.0.177
```

In the preceding example, I used the option --network to provide the network name that this new container should connect to. On the next command, I used docker inspect to check the IP address assigned to the container. As you can see, the container is using an IP address from the range I specified earlier when creating the NAT network.

Now let's look at the transparent network option. In my case, I already have a transparent network from the external virtual switch that I actually created on Hyper-V Manager for my VMs. This same external virtual switch is shown here:

```
PS C:\> docker network ls
NETWORK ID          NAME                DRIVER              SCOPE
9d3c7a5fcc99        External Network    transparent         local
49ad25853dcb        nat                 nat                 local
91a6ec72874c        none                null                local
```

When inspecting the network, you'll notice one main difference:

```
PS C:\> docker network inspect "External Network"
[
    {
        "Name": "External Network",
        "Id": "9d3c7a5fcc99a6e136a7a26dea199ddbf2b4d0cdf7da21f5a2621f
        9bd38a093a",
        "Created": "2020-08-03T12:27:05.096444-07:00",
```

```
        "Scope": "local",
        "Driver": "transparent",
        "EnableIPv6": false,
        "IPAM": {
            "Driver": "windows",
            "Options": null,
            "Config": [
                {
                        "Subnet": "0.0.0.0/0"
                }
            ]
        },
        "Internal": false,
        "Attachable": false,
        "Ingress": false,
        "ConfigFrom": {
            "Network": ""
        },
        "ConfigOnly": false,
        "Containers": {},
        "Options": {
            "com.docker.network.windowsshim.hnsid": "5012E328-995B-44C3-
            8320-322E819C8EA6",
            "com.docker.network.windowsshim.networkname": "External
            Network"
        },
        "Labels": {}
    }
]
```

As you can guess, the main difference here (in addition to the driver being transparent, rather than NAT) is there's no subnet or gateway assignment for this network. This is because the containers connected to this network will get an IP address from the DHCP server, just like any other device connected to this network. Here's what happens when I create a new container connected to this network:

```
PS C:\> docker run -d --network "External Network" --name myextnetcontainer
vinibeerimage:v2
bfa7dc082d8a120668a286bb7ef50c41518455357f98c698b1585ae1369d4d79
PS C:\> docker inspect --format='{{range .NetworkSettings.Networks}}
{{.IPAddress}}{{end}}' myextnetcontainer
10.91.149.47
```

The preceding commands are pretty much the same as I showed with the NAT network, with the change in the --network option to use the existing "External Network" network. Also, notice that I removed the -p option as we don't need to map ports from the host in this case. By default, all incoming TCP, UDP, ICMP, and IGMP traffic will be allowed. Any other protocol is blocked. Next, in the preceding example, I used the docker inspect command again to check the IP address of the new container. The IP address now is one from the range of the DHCP server on the network my container host is connected to.

Now let's look at the process of creating a new transparent network:

```
PS C:\> docker network create --driver transparent ExternalNetwork
529521080af46a374e7a7228fcdda938758683967c121342d5bf804a880d33ec
PS C:\> docker network inspect ExternalNetwork
[
    {
        "Name": "FxternalNetwork",
        "Id": "529521080af46a374e7a7228fcdda938758683967c121342d5bf
        804a880d33ec",
        "Created": "2020-08-03T16:35:54.4319238-07:00",
        "Scope": "local",
        "Driver": "transparent",
        "EnableIPv6": false,
        "IPAM": {
            "Driver": "windows",
            "Options": {},
            "Config": [
                {
                    "Subnet": "0.0.0.0/0"
                }
```

```
            ]
        },
        "Internal": false,
        "Attachable": false,
        "Ingress": false,
        "ConfigFrom": {
            "Network": ""
        },
        "ConfigOnly": false,
        "Containers": {},
        "Options": {
            "com.docker.network.windowsshim.hnsid": "24F5D3DC-F06F-44B5-
            8264-40E32A70E376"
        },
        "Labels": {}
    }
]
```

As you can see from the preceding example, the process is very similar to the
previous one for NAT; the only difference is the driver and the fact that I did not provide
a subnet and gateway – I'm choosing to let the DHCP server do that. I could provide
the same options as in the NAT network for subnet and gateway if I wanted to provide a
separate IP range for this network.

In the preceding example, you will notice that I never specified a NIC for the network
(which translates into a virtual switch). If you ever created a virtual switch on Hyper-V,
you know that we should always specify which NIC to use. For containers, this is not
mandatory. However, if you have multiple NICs and you want to create more than one
transparent network, you need to specify which NIC to use on each transparent network.
This is how you would create the same network as earlier, but binding it to a specific NIC:

```
PS C:\> docker network create -d transparent -o com.docker.network.
windowsshim.interface=Ethernet ExternalNetwork
b6925af1d0adc4254e798ca253071fd2fd18251ed667a8b209d0267965c131d2
PS C:\> docker network create -d transparent -o com.docker.network.
windowsshim.interface="Ethernet 2" ExternalNetwork2
05c265f2a538bea76493226d8bfdb0c7a2211842edadf7739a1ae152885e413d
```

We will cover the -o option from the preceding example in more detail in the following. For now, what you need to know is that it allows you to provide more details for the driver you're using. In this case, we're adding the option on the transparent driver that calls the HNS layer, to specify which NIC to use. On the first command, we used the Ethernet NIC and on the second one the Ethernet 2 NIC.

For larger scenarios, setting up the right network type has more to do with the orchestrator you chose than actually passing on the configuration via Docker. This is because if you decide to use, for example, Kubernetes, you'd configure the JSON file for the Kubernetes deployment and the Kubernetes master node would do all the work (as earlier) on the background. However, setting up the options manually on Docker for overlay, l2bridge, and l2tunnel are pretty much the same. The syntax of the docker network create is the same, but in each case, you'd have to specify different options depending on your scenario.

Finally, there are some additional configurations you can do to support some interesting requirements. Let's take a look at some of these.

Setting up advanced configurations for networking

The HNS layer provided by the Windows OS to containers is the same one used for VMs. If you are familiar with VMs on Hyper-V, you know that the Hyper-V virtual switch evolved a lot over the years. Today, the Hyper-V virtual switch is a robust solution and not only supports advanced features but also allows for third-party plugins. In this section, we will explore some of these advanced features, but in the containers space.

Before diving into the configuration, it's important to remember that although we're managing the network configuration via Docker, everything is implemented by the HNS layer, which at the end of the day owns the drivers used by each network type. From the docker command, the way to call out the HNS layer is by adding the -o option on the docker network create command. The -o option stands for "opt map" or "option mapping" and is a way for Docker to allow you to specify a driver specific configuration without having to add new parameters to the docker command itself. The problem is that you have to know how to call out the driver-specific option, and that's why I mentioned before that you should always check with your vendor if you're using a third-party driver.

For HNS, here are some common options we can use when creating a new network.

Switch embedded teaming

On larger servers supporting production environments, we always try to avoid any single point of failure. One of these single points might be your virtual switch going offline because the NIC it's connected to has gone down – either because the NIC went down or the link went down. To avoid these scenarios, the Hyper-V virtual switch allows you to create an embedded teaming, which essentially means you can create a virtual switch that has two or more NICs to use.

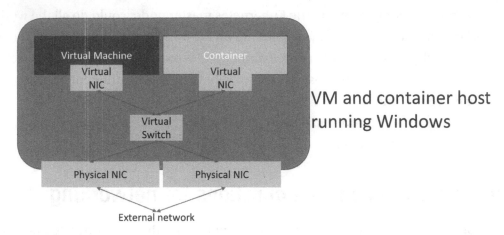

Figure 4-4. *Switch embedded teaming with two NICs*

In Figure 4-4, we see the same architecture as we discussed previously. The difference in this case is the switch is connected to two physical NICs, which allows the containers (and potential VMs connected to the virtual switch) to continue to communicate with the external network even in the event of a NIC failure.

To configure this, we'll use the same option as earlier on which we specified which NICs to use on a transparent network, but in this case, we'll add more than one NIC to the same network:

```
PS C:\> docker network create -d transparent -o com.docker.network.
windowsshim.interface=Ethernet, "Ethernet 2" ExternalNetwork
b6925af1d0adc4254e798ca253071fd2fd18251ed667a8b209d0267965c131d2
```

The preceding command will take care of creating the network on the container host, and the containers will connect to a virtual switch that transparently uses two NICs instead of just one. This applies to all network drivers.

VLAN configuration

On enterprise scenarios, the complexity of the network can overwhelm some of the networking switches and routers. To solve that, many companies adopt a network segregation strategy to create smaller chunks of networks and improve performance. The most common way to segregate networks is by using Virtual LAN Identifiers (VLAN IDs). VLAN IDs can be implemented on Hyper-V virtual switches and by containers can follow that as well. To do that, you can use this option:

```
PS C:\> docker network create -d transparent -o com.docker.network.
windowsshim.vlanid=20 ExternalNetwork
b6925af1d0adc4254e798ca253071fd2fd18251ed667a8b209d0267965c131d2
```

The preceding option will set the VLAN ID of the network (and virtual switch) to 20, which will set the VLAN isolation mode. All endpoints (container NICs) attached to this network will inherit that configuration. In addition to the preceding configuration, since all containers will be using one NIC to talk to the physical switch (the container host NIC), you need to ensure this port is configured on trunk mode.

The VLAN ID configuration here is expected to be a reflection of the physical network. Because of that, this option is only available for transparent and l2bridge.

Providing network name to HNS

This is more of a cosmetic configuration. You might have noticed that when inspecting the networks created in the preceding examples, they did not have the network name passed to the HNS layer in the options' block of the JSON output:

```
"Options": {
        "com.docker.network.windowsshim.hnsid": "24F5D3DC-F06F-44B5-
        8264-40E32A70E376"
},
```

For cases on which troubleshoot is needed on the HNS layer (usually when contacting Microsoft support), you might want to have the network name the same as the docker layer, so it makes it easier for identification purposes. To do that, you can add the following option:

```
PS C:\> docker network create -d transparent -o com.docker.network.
windowsshim.networkname=ExternalNetwork ExternalNetwork
b6925af1d0adc4254e798ca253071fd2fd18251ed667a8b209d0267965c131d2
```

This option works for all network types.

Force a network to use specific NIC

We touched this option briefly earlier when covering multiple transparent networks on the same host. In some cases, you might want to force a network to use a specific NIC – regardless of the type, expect for NAT. To achieve that, you can use the following:

```
PS C:\> docker network create -d l2bridge -o com.docker.network.
windowsshim.interface="Ethernet 2" ExternalNetwork
05c265f2a538bea76493226d8bfdb0c7a2211842edadf7739a1ae152885e413d
```

Provide DNS suffix and DNS server for a network

In previous sections, we covered that when creating a new network, we can either use a specific subnet for that network or let the DHCP server provide IP addresses for the containers. However, DHCP servers provide more than IP addresses and gateways to use. In fact, one important component that needs to be added if access to the Internet is needed on any network expecting NAT is DNS. DNS allows the OS to query for an IP address when a fully qualified domain name (FQDN), such as www.microsoft.com, is entered. If no DNS servers are available, the query will fail. For that reason, you might want to provide a DNS suffix (which is the complement of an address to be used in case hostname is provided instead of FQDN) and DNS server to be used by the containers. To do that, you can use this option:

```
PS C:\> docker network create -d transparent -o com.docker.network.
windowsshim.dnssuffix=myinternaldomain.local -o com.docker.network.
windowsshim.dnsservers=192.168.0.10,192.168.0.11 ExternalNetwork
05c265f2a538bea76493226d8bfdb0c7a2211842edadf7739a1ae152885e413d
```

The following example applies both the DNS suffix and the DNS servers to be used. The DNS suffix myinternaldomain.local will be added in case a query is made and only the hostname was provided. For example, if a query was made to Host1, the DNS client on the container will try to query for host1.myinternaldomain.local instead. The DNS servers used for this query are provided in the next option, 192.168.0.10 and 192.168.0.11.

This configuration applies to all network types, although NAT networks will use the DNS configuration on the container host if a specific configuration is not present on the container.

Wow, we covered a lot of ground in this chapter. We looked at resource management overall for containers and how it is different from traditional infrastructure and its own challenges. Then we dived into CPU and memory management and how to properly set up limits for these resources on containers to ensure the applications on top of them can have the performance you need. Next, we looked at storage, a completely different approach to what we're used to with VMs. We covered how to manage local storage on the container host and on the container and the options to provide persistent storage to containers. Finally, we entered the networking realm. Although there's an added complexity given the multiple components necessary for proper networking, we looked at the multiple options to make your containers work seamlessly with your existing infrastructure or work on the side of it or to completely isolate it.

It would be amazing if you now put all these concepts in practice. Try spinning up a new environment and mix these settings up. You'll find that it will quickly become somewhat of a mess. Lucky we have a solution to help you manage all this, and we'll explore that in the next chapter.

CHAPTER 5

Container management with Windows Admin Center

I hope at this stage you are feeling way more comfortable with Windows Containers and Docker's command line overall. I bet you'd be able to take on a project that involves Windows Containers and that you'd ace the process of setting up container hosts, ensuring the right architecture is in place for storage and networking, that you're using the appropriate isolation mode, and that you'd be able to take an existing application running on a VM and move it to a container. This is all great and an important foundation for many other aspects of managing Windows Containers.

In this chapter, I'd like to shift gears a little bit, though. So far, we used PowerShell for pretty much everything we've been doing around containers. We looked at commands such as docker run to create new containers, docker inspect to inspect existing containers and other assets, docker images to manage images, docker networks for managing networks, and so many others. We even looked at how Docker uses the JSON format to output information on the containers and other items. The fact is that most of the containers and microservices ecosystem rely on CLI tools, so learning how Docker uses its commands is just a first step.

While these commands and JSON outputs are very useful, sometimes a graphical user interface (GUI) works best for learning new concepts and operating an environment visually. Windows admins have relied on GUIs for decades. GUIs have made complex infrastructure and concepts easier, such as Active Directory, Failover Cluster, and so many others. For that reason, Microsoft has added the possibility of IT Pros to manage their Windows Containers via Windows Admin Center (WAC).

© Vinicius Ramos Apolinario 2021
V. Ramos Apolinario, *Windows Containers for IT Pros*, https://doi.org/10.1007/978-1-4842-6686-1_5

WAC is a web-based GUI tool to manage Windows Server and its roles and features, Failover Clusters, Hyper-converged Clusters, and Windows 10 machines. Overtime, WAC tends to replace existing legacy tools that rely on Microsoft Management Console (MMC). In the past few years, we have seen more and more additions to WAC's management capabilities, such as Active Directory, IIS, and so on. Before we dive into the Windows Containers capabilities of WAC, I want to quickly go over what WAC can do.

First, you can check more information and the free download of WAC here: `https://aka.ms/windowsadmincenter`.

If you are not familiar with Windows Admin Center, there are a few things you should know: WAC is a free web-based management tool composed of two main components, a gateway and a web server. These two components are installed when you deploy WAC on a machine. WAC's server side (composed of a gateway and web server) can be installed on a Windows Server or Windows 10 machine. From this server, you can manage additional instances of Windows Server, Failover Clusters, Hyper-converged Clusters, and Windows 10 machines. If you decide to install WAC on a Windows 10 machine, the management is available for the local user only. If you install it on a Windows Server machine, WAC works in what is called gateway mode, on which other users can access the WAC interface to manage the target servers.

Once installed and configured, this is what WAC looks like.

Figure 5-1. *Windows Admin Center Overview page*

In Figure 5-1, you can see the WAC's Overview page. First, notice that I installed WAC on a machine called WACDEMO-VM (notice the URL) and I'm managing that machine itself (notice the name of the targeted machine on the top left-hand corner). On the left-hand side, you can see that we have a number of icons representing an aspect of Windows management: certificates, devices, events, and so on. These items are called extensions, and WAC has native and non-native extensions, including third-party ones. Once you select an extension on the left-hand side, the main area on the center-right will show the working area of that option. In the preceding image, the selected Overview extension shows important information about the system you're targeting, such as computer name, OS, hardware configuration, as well as some real-time utilization graphics for CPU, memory, and disk. If you navigate to another extension, such as the Containers one, the page will change to reflect that.

The Containers extension on Windows Admin Center is not native, though. In order to use it, you need to install it from WAC's settings. Let's take a look at how to do that.

Set up the Containers extension on Windows Admin Center

Before you can use the Containers extension for WAC, you need to manually install it. However, you should prepare the architecture of WAC before you start doing anything else. As mentioned in the previous section, there are a number of ways to use WAC to manage your target servers – which in our case is a container host. You can install on a Windows 10 or Windows Server machine; you can install directly on the server you want to manage or on a jump server (a server that serves the purpose of management so you can get to the target server). Here's an overview on what the architecture looks like.

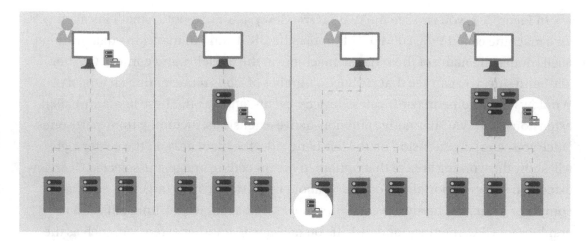

Figure 5-2. *Windows Admin Center architecture examples. Figure from*
`https://docs.microsoft.com/en-us/windows-server/manage/windows-admin-`
`center/plan/installation-options`

Figure 5-2 shows the most common installation options for WAC. From left to right,
here are the options and their pros and cons when thinking about targeting Windows
Containers:

- Install WAC on a Windows 10: This option allows you to target a
  container host and manage it remotely. However, it does not allow
  you to have other users connecting to this WAC instance. This is an
  optimal scenario for small environments or test/dev.

- Install WAC on a dedicated server: This option allows you to share
  the WAC instance with other users and have this server target other
  container hosts. While this option allows you some flexibility, it does
  require more resources, so it is recommended for production
  environments.

- Install WAC on a container host: For production environments on
  which you can't dedicate a server to WAC, you could install it on one
  of the servers running as a container host. Since WAC is very light-
  weight, it would most probably not interfere with the performance of
  your workloads. However, you should keep in mind that it could
  potentially affect your containers as WAC does have some minimal
  hardware requirements.

- Install WAC on a dedicated cluster: This is a variant of option 2 on which you might need to provide high availability to WAC itself. This should be considered an option for large scenarios and mission critical.

Finally, the other thing to keep in mind is that WAC can be installed on Server Core machines. If you have a Server Core container host and you'd like to install WAC on it to manage your containers and images, you can definitely do that. The only limitation is that you'll need to open the browser session from another machine as Server Core doesn't have a GUI/browser – which is something you should be doing anyway.

Once you decide on which topology to use, we can start the deployment of WAC itself. As mentioned, WAC is a free download tool. In order to use it, it is required that you have a valid license of Windows 10 or Windows Server. After you download the WAC package from `https://aka.ms/windowsadmincenter`, you can start the installation of the MSI package. The installation of WAC is very straightforward, and during the installation, the main information you need to provide is which port you want WAC to listen (default is HTTPS/443 on Windows Server and HTTPS/6516 on Windows 10), if you want the installation to change the Trusted Hosts in the local machine, and which certificate to use – either a self-signed or an existing one.

Before we move into the details of setup and configurations for WAC and Windows Containers, you should remember that WAC does not follow the regular update cadence of Windows Server and Windows. WAC itself has a 6-month update cadence that is not necessarily aligned with the SAC releases of Windows and Windows Server. Furthermore, extensions can be updated totally apart from WAC, and sometimes, there will be updates to them every month. For the following demonstration, I'm using the WAC version 2007, build 1.2.2007.18002. Also, I'm using the version 1.112.0 of the Containers extension. If you have a newer version of either WAC or the Containers extension, you might see a different set of features; however, the concepts must be the same.

Once you finish WAC's installation wizard, you can open a browser – either locally or remotely – targeting the address provided at the end of the installation. When you open WAC, you'll land on the "All connections" page.

Figure 5-3. *Windows Admin Center's All connections page*

By default, there's a connection to the localhost on which you installed WAC. If you installed WAC on a jump server, you can add a connection to the server you want to manage. To do that, follow the +Add button as in Figure 5-3 to add a new connection. Once you select that option, you are presented with the multiple options of connections WAC supports that we already discussed: Server, Windows PCs, Server clusters, and Azure VMs. To add a container host, simply select the Server option, and on the next step, provide the server name. Once you provide the server name, WAC will look for it, and if everything is OK, the +Add button at the bottom will enable you to add that server.

Before we open the server connection, we also need to install the Containers extension. To do that, click the Settings button on the top right-hand corner. On the Settings page, click the Extensions option under Gateway on the left-hand side menu. You'll notice the Available extensions page already shows the Containers extension option. This extension comes from the default extension feed on WAC, which is a cloud location on which Microsoft stores its available extensions for WAC. However, WAC also provides an Insiders feed on which new functionality is made available in preview. To add the Insiders feed, click the Feeds tab.

Extensions

We might have to restart the Windows Admin Center gateway after installing an extension, temporarily affecting availability for anyone else currently using this gateway.

Available extensions   Installed extensions   **Feeds**

\+ **Add**   🗑 Remove   2 Items   Search   🔎

☐ Package feeds ↑

https://aka.ms/sme-extension-catalog-feed

https://aka.ms/wac-insiders-feed

Figure 5-4. *Adding Insiders feed on Windows Admin Center*

On the Feeds tab, click the +Add button and add the `https://aka.ms/wac-insiders-feed` URL. Once you add, you'll see the new feed has been added to the Feeds page as in Figure 5-4. Now let's check the Available extensions tab again. You should see a newer version of the Containers extension available now from the Insiders feed. Select that extension and click Install. WAC should reload after the installation, and once that is completed, the extension should show up as installed on the Installed extensions tab. Whenever an update is made available to an extension you have installed, you'll see a pop-up notification from WAC letting you know an update is available. To install an update, go back to the Installed extensions page, select the extension, and click Update.

Now that we have everything in place, we can go back to the All connections page and click the server we'd like to manage. To connect remotely to that server, WAC will always use the credentials you're using on that browser session. If you are in an Active Directory environment, the credentials you use to log in will be used, and if these credentials don't have the right permissions, WAC will ask you to provide the appropriate credentials. Also, you can force WAC to use the credentials you want instead. To change the default credential used to manage a server, mark the check box close to the server name, and click Manage as to change the credentials. There you go. Now you have a fully functional WAC instance ready to manage your container host.

To see if the connection and if WAC is working properly, select the container host you want to manage, and click the Containers extension on the left-hand side list of extension available.

If you don't see the Containers extension available or if a message saying the Containers feature is not installed properly shows up when you try to manage a server, make sure the Containers feature and Docker are installed properly as we saw in Chapter 1.

If everything worked correctly, you should see the Summary page on the Containers extension as in Figure 5-5.

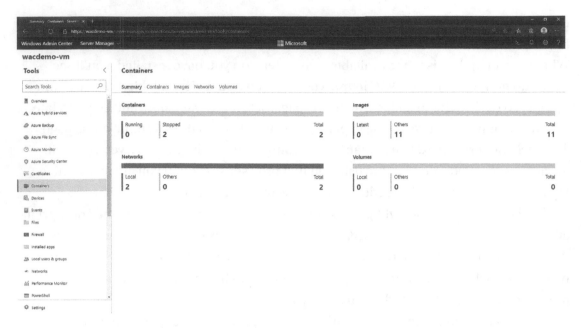

Figure 5-5.   Containers extension Summary page on Windows Admin Center

Alright, that was a lot of steps to get here. With time, you should feel more comfortable with WAC and its settings. The most important thing is that once you have WAC set up, you don't have to go through all of this again. All you have to do is add new servers and the Containers extension should show up – as long as the Containers feature and Docker are installed. Now let's dig into what we can do with WAC for Windows Containers.

Containers extension overview

A little bit of history here: the Containers extension for WAC was launched at Microsoft Ignite 2017, just one year after the launch of Windows Server 2016 on which Windows Containers were introduced. The goal of this extension has always been to provide Windows admins and IT Pros a way to manage containers running on top of container hosts. If you look at the tabs available in this extension, you'll see you have there pretty much the same components we've been talking about throughout this book. At first, most of the functionality of this extension was read-only and was intended as a way to check what's going on, but all action should go back to PowerShell. Just recently (as of the writing of this book), new functionality was added to allow an even deeper administration of container hosts, images, and containers themselves. Here's what you can do with the Containers extension on WAC:

- Containers tab: Here you can see all your containers. Think of this tab as your "docker ps -a" command on steroids. This tab allows you to see the details of each container, but also start an interactive session, check for logs and events, and so on. Here you can also stop and delete containers.

- Images tab: A nice view of all your images and more. This tab not only gives you the list of images pulled to this container host but also allows you to create new images, pull and push images, delete images, and even run new containers based on a selected image.

- Networks and volumes tabs: In Chapter 4, we covered not only the default configuration for networking and storage but also how to use alternatives better suited to your environment. In this tab, you have a read-only view of these resources and its details.

The combination of these tabs provides a powerful GUI tool to manage the lifecycle of Windows Containers. In the following sections, we will explore scenarios in which using WAC to manage Windows Containers comes in handy. The funny thing about learning how to perform these activities via WAC is that WAC itself performs the actions via Docker's CLI in the background, so you essentially know what WAC is doing in the background at this point. Learning how to perform these actions was important to gain knowledge on containers, but on a day-to-day basis, using WAC will prove to be more efficient.

Troubleshooting Windows Containers with Windows Admin Center

Let's say you have a system – don't think about VMs or containers at this point – that has an application running and users complain they get an error when performing an action, but it's not consistent; sometimes the action works, and sometimes it doesn't. What would you do? Where would you start? It depends, right? Exactly. There are way too many things to look at when it comes to troubleshooting an application and its environment. In general, you'd probably start with something like these: How is this system configured? What version of OS and application are deployed? What about the networking configuration? What about the OS and application logs? Can I remotely connect to that server to see what's going on? And so on.

With containers, the job of troubleshooting an application is a bit more complex than usual. It starts with the fact that there's no GUI. You might argue that a Server Core VM doesn't either, but in the case of a Server Core VM, you still open a remote desktop connection (usually referred to as RDP from Remote Desktop Protocol) and not only open a command line and PowerShell window but also open tools such as Perf Mon, Event Viewer, and so on. Containers don't provide that by default or at least not that easy. In fact, there's a plethora of vendors out there offering monitoring and management solutions for containers – and as you can image, mostly for Linux containers.

Figure 5-6. *Containers tab on Windows Admin Center*

So how does WAC helps here? Let's look at the Containers tab.

Right off the gate, you can see some interesting stats on the selected container. On the container line itself, we get some information such as what image this container was created from, how long has the container been running, what are its port mapping config, and so on. Next, if we look at the details pane, we get a nice Stats view showing CPU, Memory, and Network I/O. That in itself might give you some clues on what might be happening to this container or the application running on it. If you see a spike or a valley on one of these metrics and that is unexpected, it's better to take a closer look.

In the next tab, the Details tab, you can get additional information on the container and its Docker-related information. Here you can see some information from the upper pane, but some are not that easy to find, such as the Container Process ID. You can also see the Isolation type, which type of driver is being used to manage the container, which network this container is connected to (which is handy when you have multiple ones) and its IP address, and if there are any mounted volumes.

The Container Process ID shown in the Details tab is the same job object discussed in Chapter 4. Limits applied to this process ID will be inherited by the container's processes.

Next, we have the Logs tab. This tab deserves some explanation: when Microsoft launched Windows Server, version 1709, it released an experimental feature that would allow Linux containers on Windows (LCOW) natively via hypervisor isolation. Since then, Microsoft has moved away from that implementation, and today LCOW is only supported on test/dev scenarios on top of Windows 10 with Docker Desktop with a completely different approach that actually uses a full Linux VM for that. In any case, the reason I'm explaining all that is because the Logs tab calls for a Docker command called "docker logs". This command looks for an application and system log standard on Linux called Standard Output (STDOUT). On Windows, the implementation of system and event logs is completely different. Windows stores these logs as Event Tracing for Windows (ETW) and Event Logs (visible as Event Viewer) so Docker can't find any logs to show on the docker logs command, thus making this tab irrelevant for Windows containers. In the past, however, you could run an LCOW, open WAC and select that container, go to this tab, and see the docker logs. For now, we'll move to the next tab, but at the end of this section, we'll cover how to use a tool called Log Monitoring to show logs from Windows containers in this tab.

The next sub-tab in our Containers tab on WAC is the Console one. This tab is extremely useful. Earlier in the book, we looked at how to establish an interactive PowerShell session to a container instance. Question: do you remember the container by the top of your head? No, right? It's OK – at least you have this book. Another way is to just click this tab. When you open this tab, WAC will call for an interactive session with the selected container. For cases on which you want to check if a file was copied correctly, or if you need to check if a service was started, or if you want to perform any interaction action in this container, this is an easy way to do that.

Finally, we have the Events tab. Personally, this is my preferred tab. Why? Because it gives you a familiar view. Look at Figure 5-7.

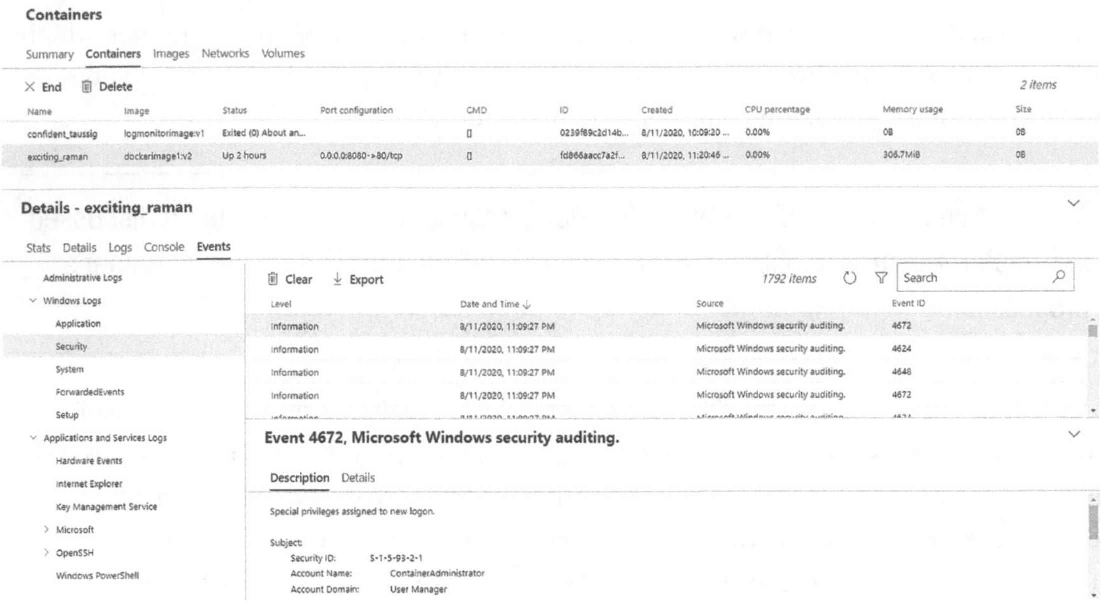

Figure 5-7.   *Events tab on Windows Admin Center*

If you ever opened Event Viewer, this should be familiar to you. Here we have all the events you'd see on Event Viewer inside this container. You can select which logs you want to check, such as Application, Security, System, and so on. You can also drill down to the Applications and Services Logs that give you a more granular list of logs from each source on Windows. Once you select a source on the left-hand side, you have the list of events on the main center-right panel. When an event is selected, the details are expanded as you can see in Figure 5-7.

The Event Viewer–like view is amazing as it provides some familiarity on how to troubleshoot a server from the details on the event logs. However, there's still the Logs tab on which you can integrate with the docker logs command. As promised, let's check how to integrate that with the Log Monitoring tool.

Integrating the Log Monitoring tool with Windows Admin Center

Going back to the Logs tab, the question is: Is this tab completely irrelevant now, since docker logs is only supported natively on Linux containers? Well, not exactly. Microsoft has recently released a new Log Monitoring tool that fills the gap on Windows and exposes the system logs and events to STDOUT. The tool is available here: `https://github.com/microsoft/windows-container-tools`.

While the utilization of the tool itself is apart from WAC, we can benefit from using it and have WAC displaying the logs, rather than using the docker logs command.

Before we dive into how to install the Log Monitoring tool, let me just recap that this tool is completely apart from WAC. In our effort to troubleshoot Windows Containers, we're showing the combination of them, but combining them is not required.

The purpose of the Log Monitoring tool is to catch the logs you'd like to see on the STDOUT format, so it shows up on docker logs. To accomplish that, the tool is composed of two parts:

- LogMonitor.exe: This executable can be downloaded from the preceding link and is the tool itself. Its job is to monitor logs on the locations and providers you specify, and translate them into the STDOUT format.

- LogMonitorConfig.json: This JSON file tells LogMonitor.exe what to monitor. It allows for the configuration of three log types: Event Logs, Custom Logs, and ETWs. Each configuration has its own pattern to be added to the JSON file. More details on how to configure each can also be found on the preceding URL.

For our example, here is a sample from the GitHub repo:

```
{
  "LogConfig": {
    "sources": [
      {
        "type": "EventLog",
        "startAtOldestRecord": true,
        "eventFormatMultiLine": false,
        "channels": [
```

```
        {
          "name": "system",
          "level": "Error"
        }
      ]
    },
    {
      "type": "File",
      "directory": "c:\\inetpub\\logs",
      "filter": "*.log",
      "includeSubdirectories": true
    },
    {
      "type": "ETW",
      "providers": [
        {
          "providerName": "IIS: WWW Server",
          "ProviderGuid": "3A2A4E84-4C21-4981-AE10-3FDA0D9B0F83",
          "level": "Information"
        },
        {
          "providerName": "Microsoft-Windows-IIS-Logging",
          "ProviderGuid ": "7E8AD27F-B271-4EA2-A783-A47BDE29143B",
          "level": "Information" ,
          "keywords": "0xFF"
        }
      ]
    }
  ]
  }
}
```

When looking closely at the preceding example, you'll notice that we have three main blocks for the configuration – the same ones discussed earlier: EventLog, File, and ETW. We added these three here for demonstration purposes, but you could either remove one of the blocks, if not needed, or add more information on each block if needed. Also, each block has a specific type of level of logs you'd like to catch – such as information, error, and warning.

Once you have both assets, you can store them in a separate folder or in the folder of the application you're containerizing. For the following example, we'll use the standard IIS image and configure the dockerfile to run a ping command so the Log Monitoring tool can catch the result of each ping attempt. Here's what the dockerfile looks like:

```
FROM mcr.microsoft.com/windows/servercore/iis:windowsservercore-ltsc2019
WORKDIR /LogMonitor
COPY . .
ENTRYPOINT C:\LogMonitor\LogMonitor.exe  c:\windows\system32\ping.exe -n 20
localhost
```

The preceding dockerfile will start with the IIS image, set the working directory to C:\LogMonitor, copy the content of the local folder (which includes both the exe and JSON files) to the destination folder in the container, and set the Log Monitoring tool as the entrypoint. Notice that when we set the entrypoint in this case, we're also calling the ping command we mentioned will be used as an example. Finally, to run the container, we could use WAC, but since we did not cover this yet, here's the docker run command that would work:

```
PS C:\LogMonitor> docker run -d -p 8081:80 logmonitorimage:v1
0239f89c2d14bf3ae01375fd017adf1f4e8f228aaacd837e6bdbfd868f6a5098
```

As you can see, there's absolutely no change to a regular docker run command. However, here's the end result on the Logs tab on WAC.

Containers

Summary **Containers** Images Networks Volumes

✕ End   🗑 Delete   *2 items*

Name	Image	Status	Port configuration	CMD	ID	Created	CPU percentage	Memory usage	Size
confident_taussig	logmonitorimage:v1	Exited (0) 45 minut...		▯	0239f89c2d14b...	8/11/2020, 10:09:20 ...	0.00%	0B	0B
exciting_raman	dockerimage1:v2	Up 2 hours	0.0.0.0:8080->80/tcp	▯	fd866aacc7a2f...	8/11/2020, 11:20:46 ...	0.00%	49.21MiB	0B

Details - confident_taussig   ⌄

Stats Details **Logs** Console Events

Logs of confident_taussig

```
2020-08-11T22:09:23.621841700Z <Source>EventLog</Source> <Time>2020-05-07T05:10:00.000Z</Time> <LogEntry> <Channel>System</Channel> <Level>Error</Level> <EventId>7023</EventId> <Message>The IP Helper service terminated with the ...
2020-08-11T22:09:23.623841700Z <Source>EventLog</Source> <Time>2020-05-12T20:28:07.000Z</Time> <LogEntry> <Channel>System</Channel> <Level>Error</Level> <EventId>7001</EventId> <Message>The srv2 service depends on the srvnet se...
2020-08-11T22:09:23.642841900Z <Source>EventLog</Source> <Time>2020-05-12T20:28:07.000Z</Time> <LogEntry> <Channel>System</Channel> <Level>Error</Level> <EventId>7001</EventId> <Message>The LanmanServer service depends on th...
2020-08-11T22:09:23.642841900Z <Source>EventLog</Source> <Time>2020-05-12T20:28:07.000Z</Time> <LogEntry> <Channel>System</Channel> <Level>Error</Level> <EventId>701</EventId> <Message>Task Scheduler service failed to start Task C...
2020-08-11T22:09:23.642841900Z <Source>EventLog</Source> <Time>2020-05-12T20:28:07.000Z</Time> <LogEntry> <Channel>System</Channel> <Level>Error</Level> <EventId>701</EventId> <Message>Task Scheduler service failed to start Task C...
2020-08-11T22:09:25.752702000Z <Source>EventLog</Source> <Time>2020-08-11T22:09:23.000Z</Time> <LogEntry> <Channel>System</Channel> <Level>Error</Level> <EventId>701</EventId> <Message>Task Scheduler service failed to start Task C...
2020-08-11T22:09:25.752702000Z <Source>EventLog</Source> <Time>2020-08-11T22:09:23.000Z</Time> <LogEntry> <Channel>System</Channel> <Level>Error</Level> <EventId>701</EventId> <Message>Task Scheduler service failed to start Task C...
2020-08-11T22:09:25.752702000Z <Source>EventLog</Source> <Time>2020-08-11T22:09:23.000Z</Time> <LogEntry> <Channel>System</Channel> <Level>Error</Level> <EventId>7023</EventId> <Message>The LanmanServer service terminated wit...
2020-08-11T22:09:33.319590800Z
2020-08-11T22:09:33.319590800Z Pinging 0239f89c2d14 [::1] with 32 bytes of data:
2020-08-11T22:09:33.319977600Z Reply from ::1: time<1ms
2020-08-11T22:09:34.325492400Z Reply from ::1: time<1ms
2020-08-11T22:09:35.328398500Z Reply from ::1: time<1ms
2020-08-11T22:09:36.330344700Z Reply from ::1: time<1ms
```

Figure 5-8. *Logs tab with logs from a Windows Container*

Figure 5-8 shows the Logs tab on WAC with logs from a Windows container, which apparently is not much, but is only possible because we configured the Log Monitoring tool to translate the Windows events into STDOUT. Here are a few things to notice from the preceding image:

- Since the logs are now coming from docker logs, not the container, we can see the logs even though the container is in the exited state.

- On the list of logs, we see logs from the Event Logs (Event Viewer) and the result of the ping command. If IIS had logged any logs into the C:\inetpub\logs folder, we'd see them here as well.

Logs vs. Events tab

So now, we looked at two options to get logs and events on Windows Admin Center, the Logs tab and the Events tab. At the end of the day, they have very similar information and purpose, but there are some differences.

Table 5-1. *Logs and Events tab comparison*

Feature	Logs tab	Events tab
Works with Windows containers	Yes, but needs to integrate with Log Monitoring tool.	Yes, works natively.
Works with Linux containers	Yes, works natively.	No. Events tab works with Windows containers only.
Logs from system events	Yes.	Yes.
Logs from application events	Yes, including non-structured STDOUT logs.	Yes, but Event Viewer application logs only.
STDOUT format (allows for third-party integration with services like Splunk, Azure Monitor, etc.)	Yes.	No STDOUT by default. Some services might be able to catch events directly from Event Viewer.

Table 5-1 is a good reference to help you understand the pros and cons of each tab. At the end of the day, my recommendation to you is: If you have Windows Containers running native features or know applications, such as IIS, SQL Server, and so on, just go with the Events tab as it will catch all logs you need by default. However, if you have an in-house developed or third-party application that writes logs to a separate folder and does not integrate with Event Viewer, then you should go with the Log Monitoring tool and the Logs tab. Another scenario on which you might want to do the Logs tab is when you have both Linux and Windows containers and you want to standardize the way you catch logs from both systems, using docker logs.

Managing Images and new containers

Now that we covered the Containers tab and its ability to help troubleshoot Windows Containers, it's time to look at the Images tab. As you know, all containers are created off a container image. Until recently (based on the writing of this book), the Images tab was pretty much a read-only view so you could check which images you had available on your container host. On the recent Insiders' updates, Microsoft added some interesting new features to help manage images, rather than just "see" what you have. Here's an overview of the Images tab.

Figure 5-9. *Images tab overview*

Here are a few things to notice in Figure 5-9: First, we have obviously a list of images available on this container host. When you select an image, the details pane on the bottom comes up showing additional information on that image. However, the most important are the actions you can perform in this tab. As you can see on top of the images, we have five buttons with actions available:

- Create New: Here we can create a new container image. The purpose of this option is to help you containerize an existing application. There are a few options available for creating new container images, and we'll cover them later in this chapter.

- Run: You can create new containers based on the selected container image. This is a great way to test if a container image you just created is working properly, for example, but also a way to simply run new container on this container host.

- Delete: Very straightforward, allows you to delete a container image. See that an error will be shown if a container based on this image is still running, so you'd have to delete the container prior to the image.

- Pull: Here you can pull container images by just giving its repository and tag.

– Push: Allows you to push a container image to an external repository. There are two options: regular registry and Azure. We'll cover these options later in this chapter.

While each preceding action can be performed separately and has its own purpose, it's when they are used together that we can see how Windows Admin Center really helps with the end-to-end experience of using containers. So let's take a look!

Lifecycle of a container image with Windows Admin Center

Let's say you have just installed a container host. As we saw since Chapter 1, it all starts with a container image, so the first thing you want to do is to ensure you have the right images available for either running containers based off them or creating new images based on those that you pulled and have available. So, the first thing you want to do is to click the Pull option.

Pulling new container images with Windows Admin Center

When clicking the Pull option, this is what you will see.

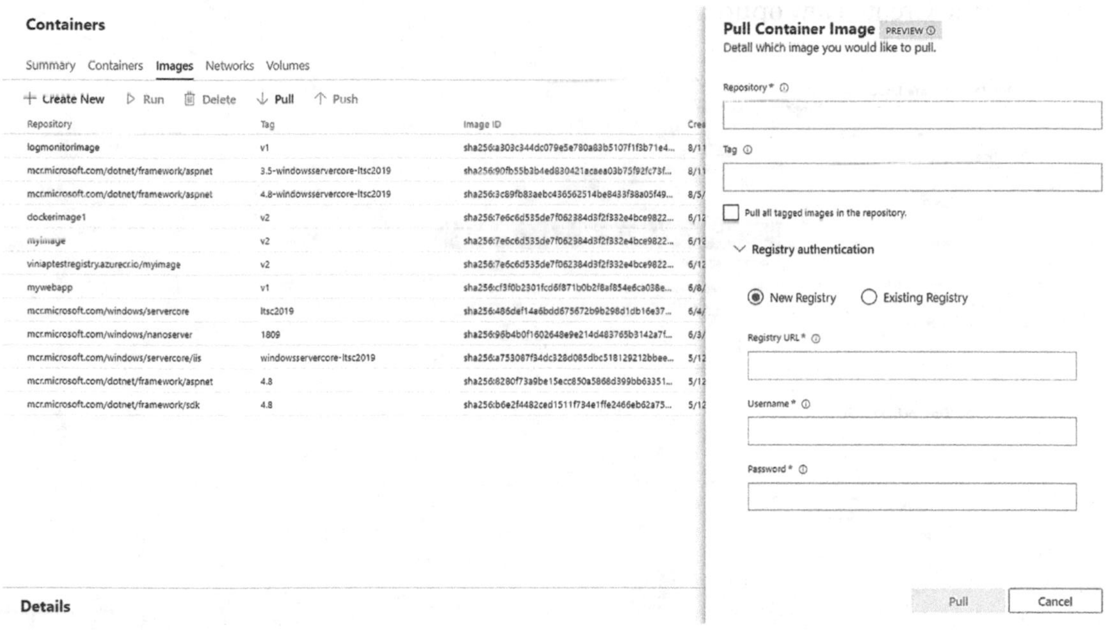

Figure 5-10. *Pulling container images with Windows Admin Center*

Figure 5-10 shows the options available for pulling a container image. Notice that I expanded the Registry authentication option and these fields are not required by default. From top to bottom, basically, you have the Repository and Tag, which are the most important information you need to pass here. This is the image you want to pull.

If the image is a public image, such as the Windows container base images, you should be good to go and clicking Pull will suffice. The authentication option is there in case you need to authenticate on that repository in order to pull the image, for example, when you have a private repository on Docker Hub. In this case, you need to provide the Registry URL, Username, and Password. If you remember from previous chapters, that's exactly what we had to use on the docker login command.

Now that you have a base container image or an image that will serve as the base for your new container images, it's time to create a new image with your application.

Creating new container images with Windows Admin Center

The Create New option is the option on the Containers extension of Windows Admin Center that I particularly like the most. The reason is that although at this point you know how to build a docker file, this option takes the pain of writing it manually away. In addition, it's easier to follow best practices. Of course, in some cases, you might need to tweak it a little bit, but most of the leg work is done for you. Here's what you see when you select the Create New option.

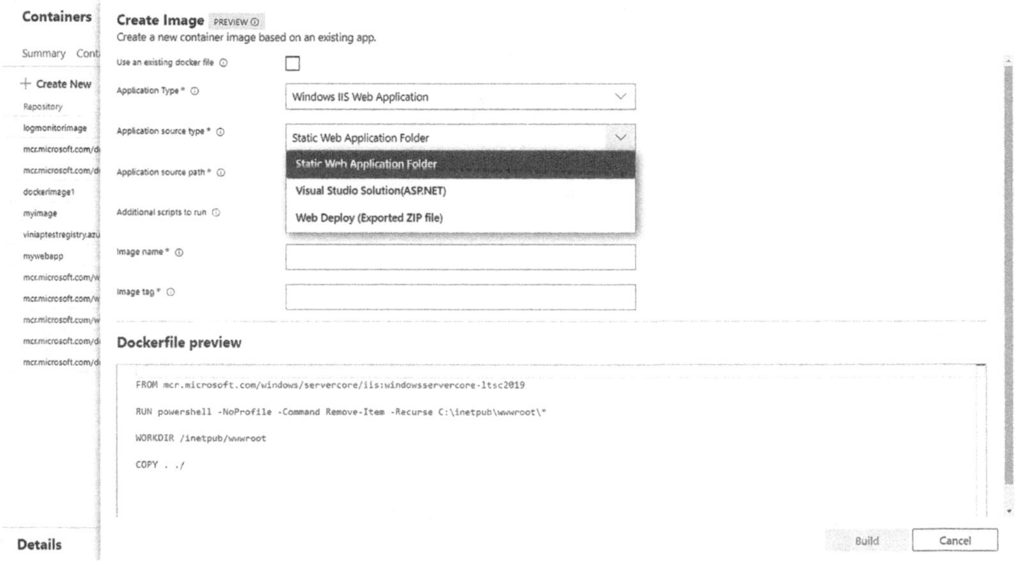

Figure 5-11. Create New images with Windows Admin Center

There are multiple options for creating new container images with WAC. Figure 5-11 shows you that the options are distributed between when you have a docker file already, different types of applications, and different application source types. Let's dig on each option:

- Use an existing docker file: This is the most basic option and can be used, for example, when you just want to re-run the docker build against an existing docker file. When you select this option, the inputs are limited to source path, image name, and image tag. When using this option, all you have to do is to pass on where your docker file is located and WAC will load it on the Dockerfile preview at the bottom. You can then either tweak the docker file or simply just build it again.

- Application Type: Here is where you select the type of application you want to containerize. As of the writing of this book, we only have one option available: Windows IIS Web Application. However, Microsoft has been updating the Containers extension constantly and has already committed to adding more application types here.

- Application source type: Here is where you say what type of source you have for that application type. Application type can be a web application, a database application, a background service application, and so on. The source type is what kind of asset you have to deploy this application again. As of the writing of this book, we have three options for our top-level IIS Web Application:

  - Static Web Application Folder: As the name says, you can use this sub-option to containerize really simple applications that only depend on a default installation of IIS. These pages don't support ASP or any other additional component. The expected source here is a folder that can then be copied to the container and used under the wwwroot default IIS folder. The base image used in this option is the generic Windows Server Core IIS image.

  - Visual Studio Solution (ASP.NET): One common scenario when containerizing an existing/legacy web ASP.Net application is to find the Visual Studio Solution left by the developer. In some cases, these applications need to be deployed on the new server (or container in our case) by restoring any framework dependencies and using Microsoft's "msdeploy". We saw this in Chapter 3 where we covered best practices with multi-staged images. This is exactly what WAC does for this source type. In addition to the path of the Visual Studio Solution, you must also specify which project you want to containerize (since the solution can have more than one project) and the framework version. The base image used in this option is the ASP.Net image.

- Web Deploy (Exported Zip File): We covered an example of containerizing web applications from Web Deploy ZIP files back in Chapter 3, and here we see that WAC can also help in that case. When using this option, you need to pass on where your exported ZIP file is located and framework version. The base image used in this option is the ASP.Net image.

– Additional scripts to run: Once you select the source type specific options, we come back to options that will apply to any type of application and source you select. The first one is the option to run an additional script. What this option will do is to simply grab a PowerShell script you might have, copy it to the base image, and execute the script at build stage. This is very helpful for applications that, in addition to deploying the application itself, you also need to perform some kind of manual or automated task. This could be creating a new folder structure, deleting logs, creating a scheduled task, adding an environment variable, or whatever you can pass on a PowerShell script.

– Image name and tag: Here you can nominate your container image so you can find it later. The name of the container image cannot contain uppercase letters.

Once you provide all the details on the image you want to create, WAC will create the preview of the docker file for you. Here's an example with the Web Deploy option.

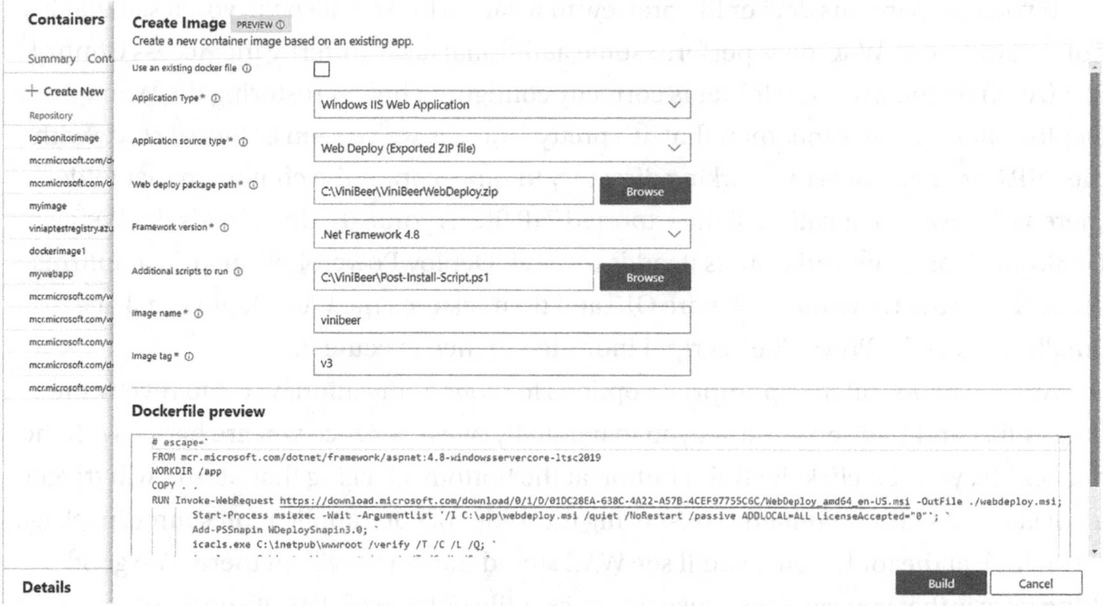

Figure 5-12. *Creating new Web Deploy–based image on Windows Admin Center*

Figure 5-12 shows the preview of a Web Deploy application being containerized. Here's the docker file preview created automatically by WAC:

```
# escape=`
FROM mcr.microsoft.com/dotnet/framework/aspnet:4.8-windowsservercore-
ltsc2019
WORKDIR /app
COPY . .
RUN Invoke-WebRequest https://download.microsoft.com/download/0/1/
D/01DC28EA-638C-4A22-A57B-4CEF97755C6C/WebDeploy_amd64_en-US.msi -OutFile
./webdeploy.msi; `
        Start-Process msiexec -Wait -ArgumentList '/I C:\app\webdeploy.msi /
        quiet /NoRestart /passive ADDLOCAL=ALL LicenseAccepted="0"'; `
        Add-PSSnapin WDeploySnapin3.0; `
        icacls.exe C:\inetpub\wwwroot /verify /T /C /L /Q; `
        icacls.exe C:\inetpub\wwwroot /reset /T /C /L /Q; `
        Restore-WDPackage -Package ./ViniBeerWebDeploy.zip

ADD Post-Install-Script.ps1 /inetpub/wwwroot
RUN powershell.exe -executionpolicy bypass c:\inetpub\wwwroot\Post-Install-
Script.ps1
```

If you compare this docker file preview to what we looked at so far, you'll see that it's not that different. WAC does perform some additional tasks to verify the Access Control List (ACL) on the wwwroot folder is correctly configured before restoring the Web Deploy package, but other than that, it's pretty much as we've seen before. It starts with the ASP.Net image, sets the working directory to /app, copies the content to that folder (here WAC uses the location of the exported ZIP file as context), downloads the Web Deploy MSI package and installs it, adds the Web Deploy PowerShell snap-in, confirms the ACLs for the wwwroot folder are OK, and then restores the Web Deploy package. Finally, it adds the PowerShell script I indicated to then execute it.

After selecting all the appropriate options for your application, you can review the docker file, and WAC even allows you to manually tweak it. Once you are happy with the docker file, you can click the Build button at the bottom. Clicking that button will trigger a docker build on the container host using the folder of your application source/package. If you look at the folder later, you'll see WAC stored the docker file in there. The good thing here is that you can now reuse this docker file outside of WAC if you want to.

When building an image via WAC, keep in mind that errors might happen just like when running docker build via Command Prompt/PowerShell. WAC will return the same error as you would see on these Shell windows. For further troubleshooting docker build, you might have to use a combination of WAC, PowerShell, and running new containers with the docker file partially built so you can see the outcome inside the container.

Once you build the image and the process works correctly, a new image will show up in your image lists. You can now click this image and check its details and also run a new container based on that image.

Running new containers via Windows Admin Center

Now that you have your image ready to go, it's a good idea to ensure the application is working properly. For that, we can use WAC and the Run option.

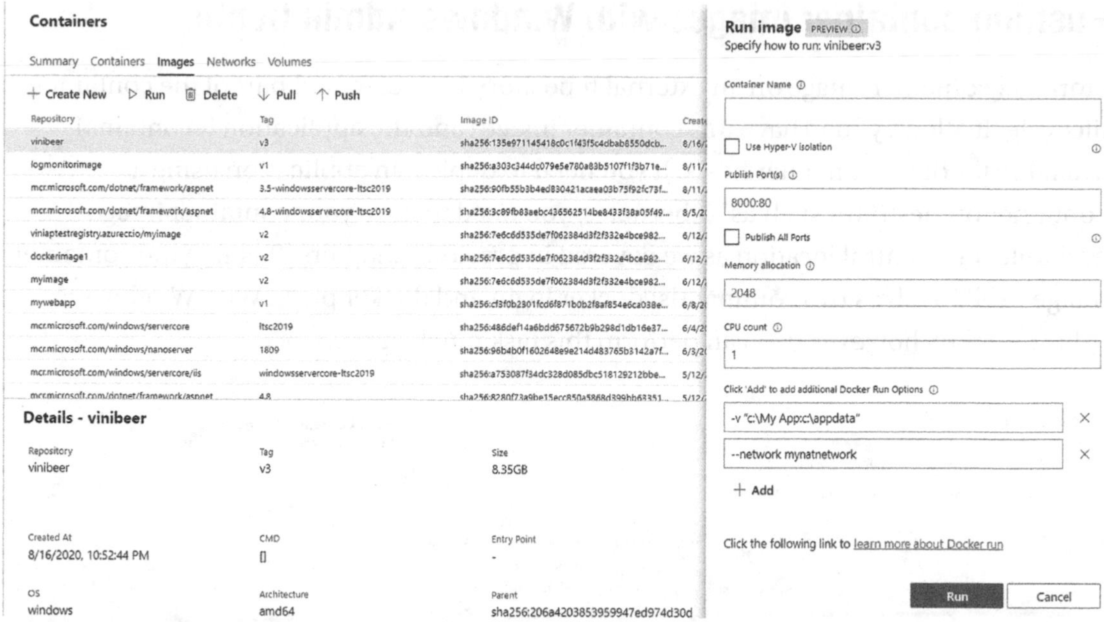

Figure 5-13. *Running new containers via Windows Admin Center*

When you select the image and click Run, the side panel shown in Figure 5-13 shows up. Here you can specify how to run this image. Notice that none of these options are required – simply clicking Run runs the image with the default docker run -d. However, there are a few things pre-populated for you, such as container name, which isolation type to use, which ports to publish (or select the option to publish the ports on the docker file), and how much memory and CPU to allocate to the container. As you know at this point, the docker run command accepts way more options than that. That's why you have the +Add button after CPU count. In Figure 5-13, I added two additional parameters to specify a mount point and which network to use. These are not pre-populated on WAC, but I can still add the values. Once you're satisfied with the options, you can click Run. The container will start, and you can then use the Containers tab to manage it as we saw in the previous section of this chapter.

Now that we validated the application on our container runs as we wanted it to run, we can push it somewhere else so another container host can run the same container.

Pushing container images with Windows Admin Center

Storing a container image on an external repository is an essential part of the container lifecycle. It allows you to have this container image (and the application it contains) available for other container hosts. If you need to deploy an application using a container orchestrator such as Kubernetes, you need to have your container image available on a central location as we covered in previous chapters. Pushing the container image itself involves two commands: docker login and docker push. With Windows Admin Center, however, you can perform this task much easily.

Figure 5-14. *Pushing container images with Windows Admin Center*

Once you select the image and click the Push option, the side panel in Figure 5-14 shows up. Here you have the option where you want to push your image to:

- Azure Container Registry: This option will use the Azure account used during the configuration of WAC connection with Azure. Different than docker login, this process does not store anything on the container host. In addition to that, before pushing the container image, you can select which subscription to use and which registry on that subscription you want to push the image to.

For more details on how to configure WAC to connect to Azure services, check the documentation page: `https://docs.microsoft.com/en-us/windows-server/manage/windows-admin-center/azure/azure-integration`.

 – Registry: This is the traditional docker login option just like we saw on the Pull option. Here you can use the credential again to log into your Docker Hub repository, for example. Just like with the Pull option, once you log into a registry, that credential is stored so you don't have to log into the registry every time you want to push it. On the flip side, however, keep in mind that as we saw in previous chapters, docker login does not store your credentials with encryption by default. Since WAC is only a cover for the docker commands, you need to configure your server to store the credentials for docker login separately.

A nice feature here before you push the container image is that you can also rename the container and its tag before pushing. Once you've selected the appropriate options, you can click Push and WAC will start the process of pushing the image to the destination you selected.

With the conclusion of pushing the image to an external registry, we went through the lifecycle of a container image on a container host: pulling container images, creating new container images, running new containers, and pushing container images. While we saw how to do this via command line in previous chapters, using Windows Admin Center provides a nicer way to perform these actions and makes it easier for you to focus on the activity, not the commands to perform them. Of course, knowing what's happening in the background is an important part of it, so if something goes wrong, you know what's happening or where to look.

At this point, there's not much more I can tell you about the foundation of Windows Containers and Docker. You are perfectly capable of running your own projects, and from now on, you'll gain knowledge by going through the cycle of a new project that involves containers and the specifics of your applications and environment. However, as I mentioned before, the ecosystem of containers is huge. There are tools for literally everything, and in the next chapter, we'll cover some of the Azure services that you can use that will help you expand the capabilities of Windows Containers and support more deployment scenarios.

CHAPTER 6

Moving your containers to the Cloud with Microsoft Azure

What a journey so far, right? If you knew nothing about containers when you started this book, you should feel proud now. I'm positive at this point you can face the challenge to go through a project that includes containerizing an existing application with Windows Containers. So far, you learned so much on this platform, and there's not much to cover from an infrastructure standpoint in regard to how Windows Containers work, how to deploy it, how to containerize an application, how to manage the container platform itself, and so on.

However, you'll also realize when using Windows Containers that most likely your project will rely on other tools and services. If you think about it, the container platform is the foundation to get your app up and running in this model. However, there are other important components that should be considered when planning for containers – much like anything else. Most of these are in regard to orchestration, but one important aspect is "Where are you going to run your application: on-premises or in the cloud?"

Of course, the answer to that question requires that a multitude of aspects to be analyzed, such as infrastructure cost, network latency, regulations, return on investment (ROI), company preference, and so much more. I can't tell you without knowing these aspects if you should run your project on-premises or in the cloud. What I can tell you is that running your container workload in the cloud comes with a lot of advantages. In this chapter, we will look at some of these when you're running your environment on Microsoft Azure.

Before we dive into each service, how it works, and how to set it up, I have one disclaimer: each of these services could have its own dedicated book about it with all the details and so on. For the purpose of this book, we will cover the important aspects of

© Vinicius Ramos Apolinario 2021
V. Ramos Apolinario, *Windows Containers for IT Pros*, https://doi.org/10.1007/978-1-4842-6686-1_6

how the service works, how to configure it so you can start using it, and some important notes about that service and Windows Containers. I'd highly encourage you to look at the documentation of each service to learn more about it if you find it interesting. You can find the docs to each of the services in this chapter at `https://docs.microsoft.com`. Finally, each of these services can be deployed and configured via different modes:

- Azure Portal: The simplest way to configure an Azure service. The Azure Portal allows for a great way to learn how a service works as there are hints all over the place. It's also a great way to monitor services that are running as the portal provides amazing graphics and detailed information about each monitored instance. To access the Azure Portal, go to `https://portal.azure.com`.

- Azure CLI and Azure PowerShell: Both of these options are command-line interfaces to manage Azure resources. These are great tools when you are comfortable managing Azure services and when you want to automate some repetitive processes. Typically, you can install the Azure CLI or PowerShell modules by downloading the installer from the Azure website: `www.azure.com`.

- Azure Cloud Shell: Another CLI option, but in this case, the Cloud Shell is executed remotely directly into the Azure API. When running an Azure Shell session, you are directly connected to Azure. The advantage here is that you don't need to install a module, such as CLI and PowerShell. You can use the Shell from a variety of ways, but the most common is `http://shell.azure.com`.

In this chapter, we will be using the Azure Portal for all demonstrations when possible. The reason for that is because the portal provides the most didactic way to understand a concept when familiarizing yourself with an Azure service. After that, you can leverage what you learned and apply it on the CLI options. With that, let's dive into some Azure fun!

Windows Containers and Azure Container Registry

We covered the importance of container registries throughout this book. Once you have a container image, the logical next step is to push it to some place it can be consumed by other container hosts or services that support containers.

Microsoft Azure offers a container registry service called Azure Container Registry (ACR). Although this chapter is all about Azure and running containers in the cloud, ACR can be used to store your container images for container hosts wherever they reside, including other clouds. As we've seen previously, if you can run the docker pull command, you should be able to download an image from a container registry to that container host.

In addition to being a container registry for storing your container images, ACR provides some cool features for managing those images. The most notable one is called ACR Tasks. ACR Tasks allow you to automate some actions, such as updating the container image with a new base OS for patching and updating. With that, let's take a look at how to get ACR up and running.

On the Azure Portal, navigate to Create a resource and look for Container Registry. On the Overview page, click Create.

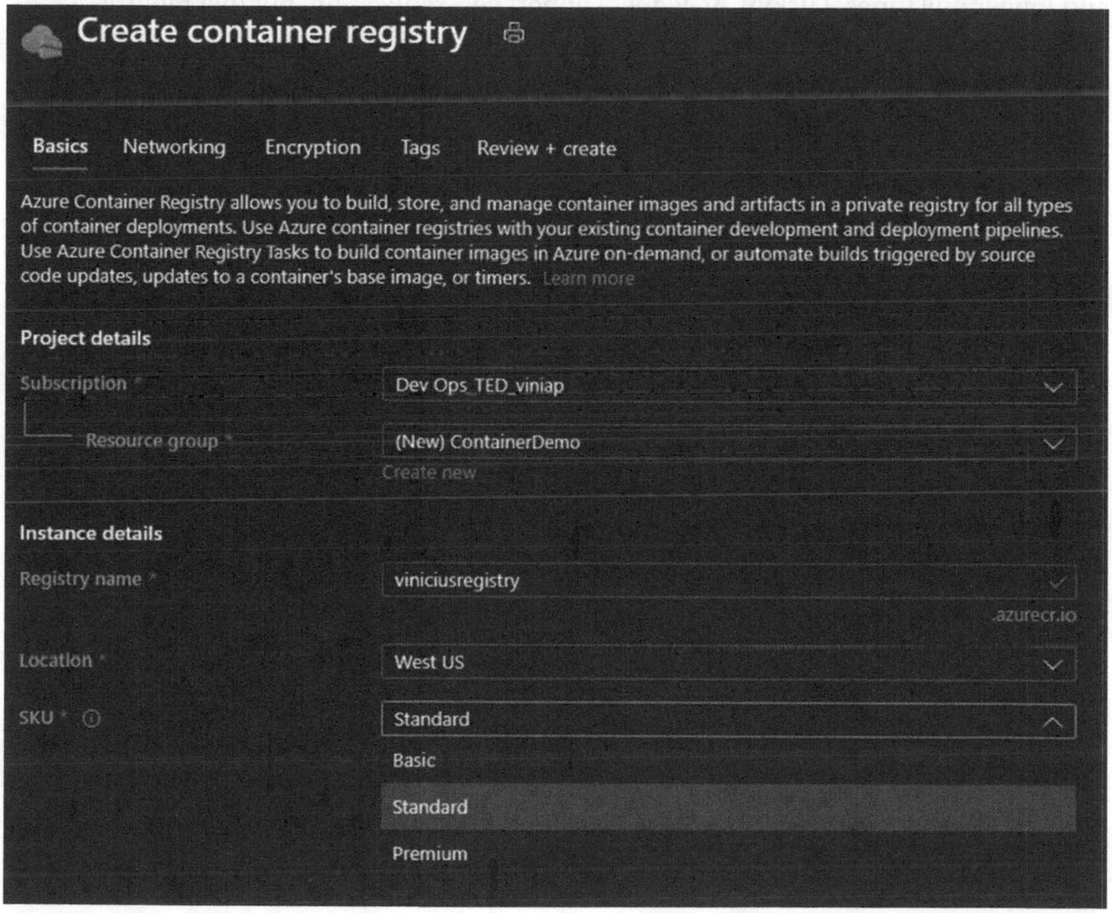

Figure 6-1. ACR creation basics

Figure 6-1 shows the initial configuration for any regular Azure service that you'll see later in this chapter. For ACR, first we need to identify our Azure Subscription which is a financial boundary in Azure. All resources under a subscription will incur charges to that subscription. You might have more than one subscription depending on how your company configured its services to be utilized. Subscriptions can also work as a security boundary for role-based access control (RBAC) or policy enforcement to apply settings to all resources on that subscription.

Once you specify your subscription, you can select the Resource group, which is used to group items that are usually co-related, such as resources that serve the same application. Next, we need to provide our registry a name, and that must be unique as the name will be used as part of the URL to access the registry. Finally, we have the location and SKU. The location of your registry is important as it determines where your container hosts will pull the image from. Far away locations will result in higher latency and longer pull times. Luckily, ACR does support geo-replication, but that requires a certain SKU.

On the SKU option, we have Basic, Standard, and Premium. There are no technical differences between the Basic and Standard SKUs, although the Standard tier provides additional storage included and better image throughout for faster push and pull operations. The Premium SKU does provide additional capabilities such as Virtual Network (vNET) integration, which allows container hosts on Azure to pull container images directly from their vNET resulting in faster pull times, geo-replication to make your image available across the globe, among other things. Once you select the region and SKU, you can click Next.

In the Networking tab, you'll be able to configure how you want the Network connectivity to work. If you selected the Premium SKU, you can either configure Public Endpoint which allows all networks to access this registry or Private Endpoint for vNET integration as discussed earlier.

Next, we have encryption which is another Premium SKU feature. Note that all content pushed to ACR is encrypted. What this option does, if available depending on your SKU selected, is to allow you to set your own customer-managed key for data at rest encryption. This option requires you to configure a "User assigned managed identity" and a key either from Azure Key Vault or a Key URI. These concepts are out of the scope of this book and should be carefully planned. Check the Azure documentation at `http://docs.microsoft.com` to learn more about it.

Finally, we have the Tags tab on which you can add value pairs of Name and Value for tags associated with this container registry. On Azure, Tags allow you to quickly identify resources as well as apply policies. Once you configure your Tags, you can click Next and check the Review + create page. If the validation passed, you'll be able to click the Create button and start the process to create your container registry.

Once your registry was created, you can check its status and configuration by navigating to that resource on the Azure Portal. As mentioned previously, there are many configurations and possibilities in terms of managing a registry on ACR. Our goal here is to get it up and running so we can push a local image to this registry. To do that, let's navigate to the Access keys tab under Settings.

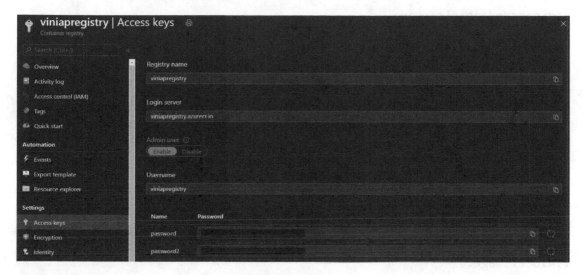

Figure 6-2. *Access keys management on ACR*

The Access keys tab allows you to configure admin access to your registry. By default, your registry is blocked for regular users authenticating with docker login. Only users authenticating via the CLI options can push images to your registry. In order to allow users to push images via the docker push command, we need to enable Admin user in this tab. Once you do that, you'll be presented with the username and two password options.

The two password options for the same user are here in case you need to audit access, since there's no option for adding multiple users under Access keys.

In Figure 6-2, we need to take note of three items: Login server, Username, and either of the passwords. With that information, we can run the docker login command on our container host:

```
PS C:\> docker login viniapregistry.azurecr.io -u viniapregistry -p
<password removed>
WARNING! Using --password via the CLI is insecure. Use --password-stdin.
WARNING! Your password will be stored unencrypted in C:\Users\viniap\.
docker\config.json.
Configure a credential helper to remove this warning. See
https://docs.docker.com/engine/reference/commandline/
login/#credentials-store

Login Succeeded
```

As you can see, the command executed successfully, but there's a warning message just like we saw when we covered docker login in previous chapters. With the login successful, we can push the image, but first we need to ensure the image matches the naming convention of that registry. Here's an example:

```
PS C:\> docker images
REPOSITORY            TAG          IMAGE ID          CREATED            SIZE
vinibeerimage         v1           10eb7bf69100      2 months ago       5.51GB
PS C:\> docker tag vinibeerimage:v1 viniapregistry.azurecr.io/
vinibeerimage:v1
PS C:\> docker push viniapregistry.azurecr.io/vinibeerimage:v1
The push refers to repository [viniapregistry.azurecr.io/vinibeerimage]
19b8ef0674a8: Pushed
902eb7282ebb: Pushed
3b3d9bfe1ae7: Pushed
4b53c5e0129b: Pushed
630f5d9ab0d6: Pushed
2334097577d8: Pushed
30b0a8f3b24d: Pushed
a7b3aa6cce02: Pushed
```

```
8bc71339d58d: Skipped foreign layer
c4d02418787d: Skipped foreign layer
v1: digest: sha256:b82f6061cfc928865c225a7d53edeab76631c1c5a6e7c751faa6875e
92c04412 size: 2783
```

To explain the preceding code, we first checked the images available with docker images. Then we used the docker tag command to tag the vinibeerimage:v1 image into the right format for our registry, which includes the ACR registry URL. Next, we used the docker push command to push that image with the appropriate tag to ACR.

You'll notice the "Skipped foreign layer" on the results of our push operation. This happens because we're using Windows base container images, and according to Microsoft's legal documentation for Windows containers, the base images cannot be redistributed.

As you know, there's another way to do this process – Windows Admin Center. With WAC, we can simply navigate to the Images tab on the Containers extension, select the image we want to push (no need to rename it), and click the Push option. Then all we have to do is to provide the same information and click Push.

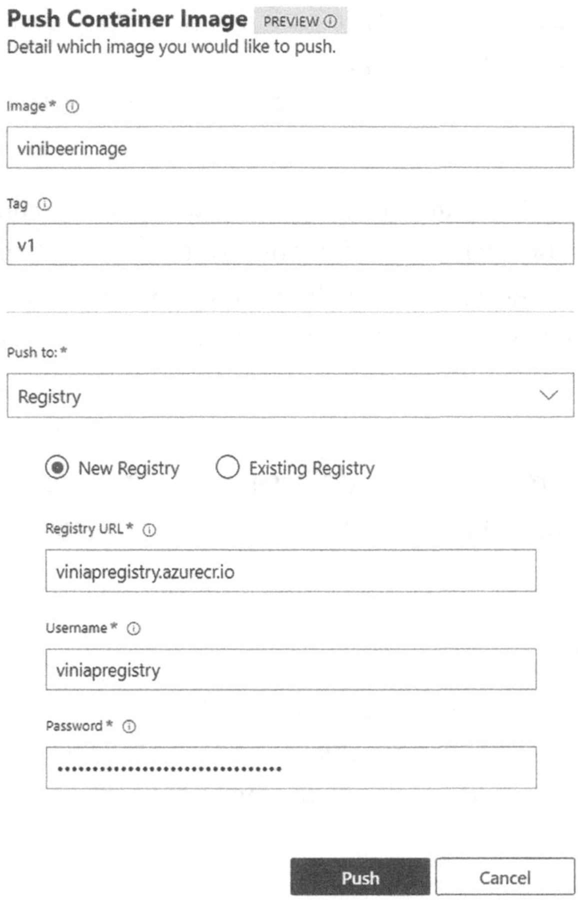

Push Container Image PREVIEW ⓘ
Detail which image you would like to push.

Image * ⓘ

```
vinibeerimage
```

Tag ⓘ

```
v1
```

Push to: *

```
Registry                                              ⌄
```

◉ New Registry   ○ Existing Registry

Registry URL * ⓘ

```
viniapregistry.azurecr.io
```

Username * ⓘ

```
viniapregistry
```

Password * ⓘ

```
••••••••••••••••••••••••••••••
```

[Push] [Cancel]

Figure 6-3. *Pushing a container image with WAC*

In Figure 6-3, you can see we're using the same parameters as docker login and docker push to push the image. The convenience here is just that we have nicer UI to do that. However, WAC also provides the option to authenticate using your Azure account, rather than the Access keys we discussed before. The difference will be that using your Azure account, WAC will show the registries available and you can select to which one you want to push it. Regardless of the option, once you fill out the forms, you can push the image.

Now let's check our image on ACR. To do that, navigate to the Repositories tab under Services.

Figure 6-4. *Checking image recently pushed to ACR*

As shown in Figure 6-4, the image is now available on our ACR registry. We can use the docker pull command to pull it on another container host. Keep in mind that, by default, ACR also blocks pull operations for non-authenticated users, so the authentication either with the Azure account or docker login is still needed. However, once we do that, we can run the following:

```
PS C:\> docker pull viniapregistry.azurecr.io/vinibeerimage:v1
v1: Pulling from vinibeerimage
65014b3c3121: Already exists
eac6fba788c9: Already exists
71ac5891d8f6: Already exists
5ff6f3d1fce7: Already exists
1778fe22ba9e: Already exists
e6754f9530cb: Pull complete
058132278c23: Pull complete
bcf7d099b897: Pull complete
5310a078bd20: Pull complete
d8a66cebd044: Pull complete
Digest: sha256:b82f6061cfc928865c225a7d53edeab76631c1c5a6e7c751faa6875e9
2c04412
```

```
Status: Downloaded newer image for viniapregistry.azurecr.io/
vinibeerimage:v1
viniapregistry.azurecr.io/vinibeerimage:v1
```

The preceding command pulled the image from the ACR registry to another container host, and now our application can be deployed just like it was on the host we built it.

With WAC, we also have the option to pull images.

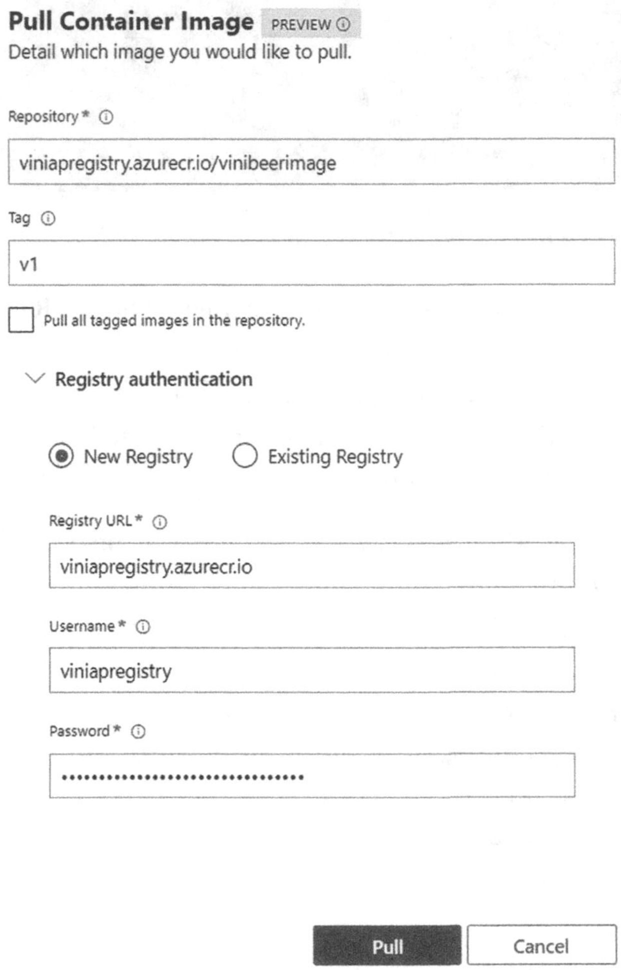

Figure 6-5. *Pulling container images with WAC*

Again, Figure 6-5 shows that the same process we did with docker commands can be accomplished using the WAC UI.

Now that you know how to create a container registry on ACR, we can start using our images on multiple hosts. In fact, the topic of our next section is exactly that: you can run your container hosts on Azure with Azure VMs! Let's see what's special about that.

Windows Containers and Azure virtual machines

You might argue: Aren't Azure VMs the same as VMs on-premises in regard to running them as a container host? Well, not quite.

From a pure OS perspective, yes. Windows Server (and Windows) runs pretty much the same on-premises and in the cloud. The difference here is in the details of the platform. First, Azure provides a marketplace of pre-configured OS images with a multitude of OS images that were prepared for container scenarios. More specifically, Microsoft publishes a few images that have the Containers feature enabled and Docker installed. Plus, these images come with the Server Core and Nano Server (and Windows in some cases) images pre-populated so you don't have to wait for the pull of these layers. The cherry on the top of this is that the OS image is updated every month to include security fixes and patches for both the container host OS and container images. Let's take a look.

On the Azure Portal, navigate to the option of creating a new resource and select Virtual Machines. On the search bar, type Windows Server with containers. You should see a list of images – some from Microsoft and some from other vendors. Change the view to list view so you can expand the list of images. You should see a long list of images under Windows Server.

Figure 6-6. *Windows Server images on Azure Marketplace*

Figure 6-6 lists all the Windows Server images on Azure Marketplace (almost all of them; the scroll would be longer than that). What you should notice on this image is the "with containers" option that is presented. Notice that since Windows Server 2016, Microsoft provides a version of the OS in the marketplace with the characteristics we just discussed. When you create a VM using these pre-configured images, they are all ready to go!

Another aspect you might have noticed is that there are also images with the [smalldisk] prefix. These images have a virtual disk of 30GB for the OS vs. the regular 127GB from regular images. This option is available for customers who deploy Server Core images and don't need a larger virtual disk for the OS. The negative here is that the pre-populated container images also consume some space, so in these OS images for the container host, the Windows base container image is not available – only the Server Core and Nano Server container images.

Finally, the option "with containers" is available on LTSC and SAC releases. For SAC as you know, the only option is to deploy the container host as a Server Core installation. For LTSC, however, you can deploy either as a regular server with desktop experience or Server Core. At this point, I don't think I need to convince you on the advantages of Server Core (smaller footprint, smaller attack surface, etc.).

Here is what a new [smalldisk] Windows Server, version 2004, with containers looks like:

```
PS C:\> docker images
REPOSITORY                                TAG    IMAGE ID      CREATED       SIZE
mcr.microsoft.com/windows/servercore      2004   e157581737ec  10 days ago   4.18GB
mcr.microsoft.com/windows/nanoserver      2004   25bef4c08869  10 days ago   262MB
The preceding images came with the VM I created - no need to pull these images.
```

That is already a big help in getting started but is not all. Azure also provides some infrastructure services that are a big help for container scenarios when it comes to VM management. To explain the feature, though, I must explain the problem first.

As an IT Pro, you are probably familiar with this dilemma: How do I update my servers regularly and still keep my applications up and running? In other words, how do I deal with reliability when my servers are being patched and rebooted?

Usually, we use a farm of servers configured in high availability (HA) and/or load balance. HA is usually used for stateful applications and load balance for stateless. In the case of HA, you move (also known as planned failover) the workload off a node (also known as evicting a node) so you can update the node, restart it, and move (planned failover again) the workload back. For load balancing, we usually reserve a minimum of nodes that need to be online all the time to support the requests to the applications and update the server farm in small chunks.

In the containers world, as long as you have enough instances of your applications, you should be OK (granted that load balancing is properly configured for the container instances). That's because you don't really care about the container host – as long as it can run that container image you created with your app. With containers, if you take a container host down, patch or update it, then bring it up, and join the farm of servers supporting your containers, you should be good. However, dealing with that manually is still a laborious process. On Azure, however, you can rely on some infrastructure features to do this for you.

The feature in Azure to help here is called Automatic VM update. Whenever you create a VM in Azure today, you have the option to say if you want additional availability options for the applications (in our case, containers) that will run on top of a set of VMs. That is called Availability set. The Availability set is an Azure configuration that creates a set of VMs behind a load balancer, and all requests are balanced to the VMs behind it. Here is the moment while creating a new VM when you select the Availability set.

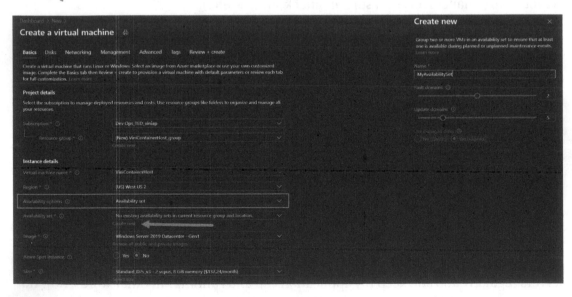

Figure 6-7. *Creating a new VM with Availability set*

In Figure 6-7, we have the traditional page to create a new VM. One of the options there is the availability, and we selected Availability set. Since we don't have any created, we can click the "Create new" button, and that brings the sidebar on which we specify name and the following:

- Fault domain: VMs in the same fault domain will share the same power and networking switch source. While having VM proximity is good to provide better performance, it also means these VMs will be offline in case of a datacenter failure. When you create more than one fault domain and multiple VMs in the same Availability set, Azure will separate these VMs in different racks to avoid disruptions to the application.

- Update domain: VMs in the same update domain are restarted together when there's a planned maintenance or when Automatic OS image upgrade kicks in. By creating multiple update domains, we ensure Azure will never turn off VMs on different update domains at the same time.

For our scenario, you can tell Azure to configure an Automatic OS image upgrade per Availability set. What Azure will do is track from which image your VMs were created, and whenever an update to that image is available, Azure will start the process of updating it. To ensure the workloads are not affected, Azure will only update a maximum of 20% of the VMs each time. Until the initial set of VMs is back up, the remaining 80% of the VMs in that Availability set is not touched. To configure Automatic OS image upgrade, you need to run the following command against a specific Scalability Set (there's not UI option in the Azure Portal):

```
PS C:\> Update-AzVmss -ResourceGroupName ViniContainerHost_group
-VMScaleSetName MyAvailabilitySet -AutomaticOSUpgrade $true
```

The preceding PowerShell command will mark the Availability set we created in Figure 6-7 to use Automatic OS image upgrade.

However, there is one gotcha here: the way this feature works under the hood is it replaces the OS disk for that VM with a new version of the image from which the VM was created. That means all configuration is lost in that process. You'd need to reconfigure the application – in our case, the containers – again when the process is over. There are two ways to solve that:

- The most basic option is to simply configure a desired state on a script and run that script once the upgrade completes – not a very elegant solution but very efficient. In fact, Azure has some resources to run scripts on a VM so it wouldn't be that hard. The script would look like the following:

    - Step 1: Pull the image you need to run (remember, Docker is already installed and ready to go).

    - Step 2: Ensure the configuration on the host is OK to support that container image (remember all the things we looked at in this book, such as storage, networking, gMSA, etc.).

    - Step 3: Run a container based on the image you just pulled.

- The most complex but way more elegant option is to use two other Azure features: Azure Image Builder and Azure Shared Image Gallery. Here's what they do:

    - Azure Image Builder allows you to programmatically create a new VM image. All steps on configuring the VM should be executed via script, and the end result is an image with all the configurations you need – including the customization we just described in the preceding steps.

    - Azure Shared Image Gallery: Instead of using the image from the public Azure Marketplace, you can have your own gallery of VM images to use. In addition to having only images you created, you can configure Azure Image Builder to use it as a location store.

The combination of creating your own image with Image Builder, then storing the image on the Shared Image Gallery to then deploy VMs from it, and configuring an Availability set might seem a bit complex, but is extremely powerful. The end result is a totally automated process in which when a new version of the image you created is put in your Shared Image Gallery, the upgrade of the VMs starts right away and you don't have to do anything – other than ensuring the containers are up and running.

Still, running containers on VMs directly does require a lot of maintenance and that you manage a lot of the infrastructure that doesn't necessarily add value at the end of the day. Unless you really need to granularly configure the VMs, the next sections should provide a way easier option to run containers on Azure.

Windows Containers and Azure Container Instances

If you are looking for a way to simply run a container based on a container image, there's no easier way than Azure Container Instance (ACI). As the name says, this Azure service runs an instance of a container for you. That's it. You don't have to worry about the infrastructure at all. In fact, you don't even have access to the container host when using ACI. When the container runs, you can select how much memory, CPU, and some other basic configuration for your container, but that's about it. While the process is extremely simple, the downside of it is that there's no orchestration here and you can't scale your app to use more containers. Still, if that satisfies your scenario, ACI is a great option. Let's see how to set it up. On the Azure Portal, navigate to the option to create new resources and type container instance.

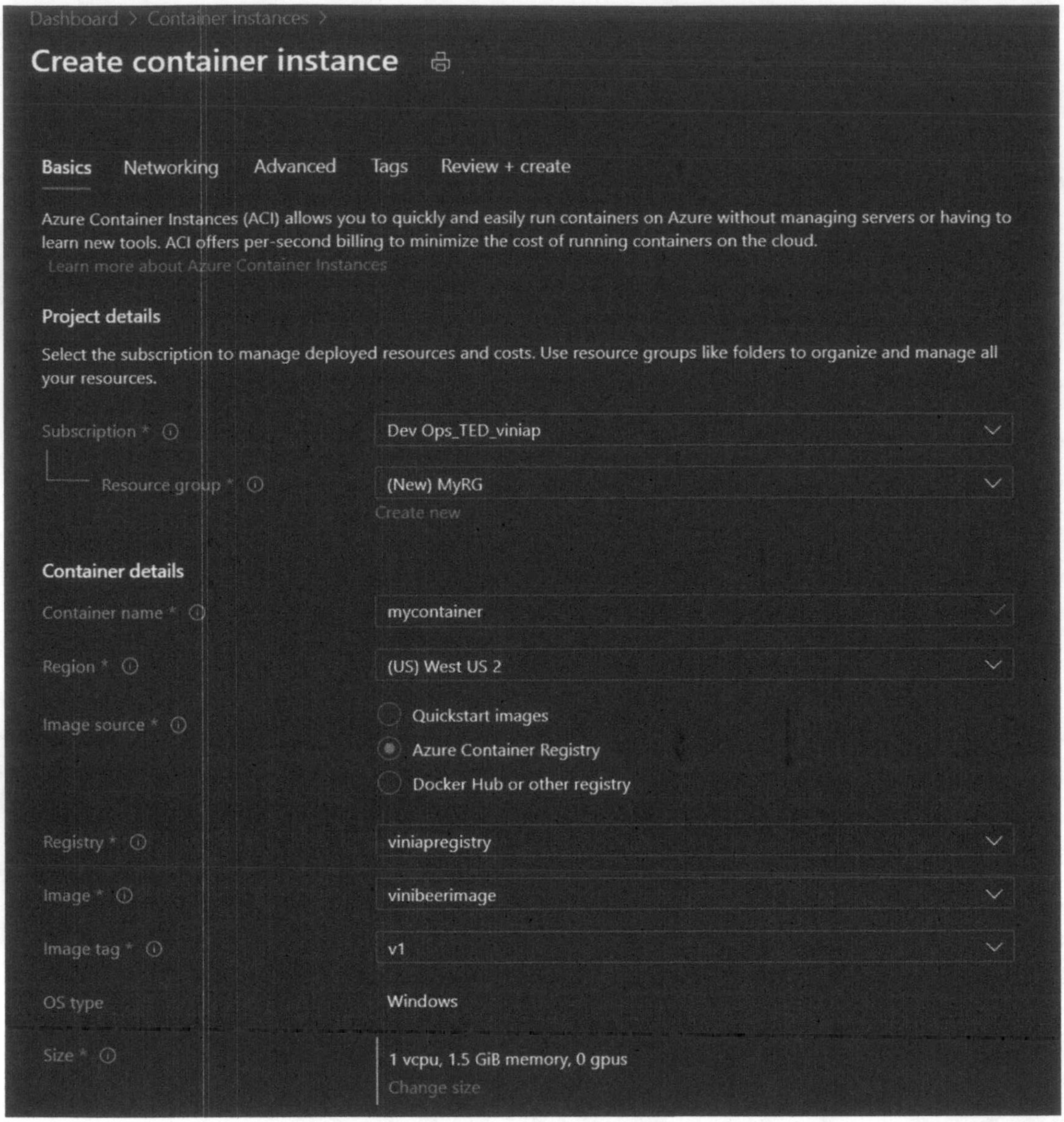

Figure 6-8. *Creating a new container instance on Azure Container Instances*

On the Basics tab shown in Figure 6-8, we have the initial configuration of our container instance. Here you have regular Azure settings, such as Subscription and Resource group. We can also set up the container name, the region it's going to run, and which image to use. On the Azure Portal, ACI provides three options:

- Quickstart images, which gives you some Hello World examples to use.

- Azure Container Registry, which lists the ACR registries available in the same subscriptions and the images on each registry. The authentication here happens directly – just remember to set up Access keys as we saw in the "Windows Containers and Azure Container Registry" section of this chapter.

- Docker Hub or other registry, which will ask you for the regular URL, username, and password for the image you want to use – unless it's a publicly available image.

Then we have the OS type, which in the case of ACR is loaded automatically. Next, we have the Size, and as any Azure compute resource, this will dictate how much you'll pay hourly/monthly for that container instance.

If you click Next, you get to the Networking page. Unfortunately, at this moment vNET integration is not available for Windows Containers. On the Advanced tab, we have the Restart policy that allows you to tell Azure when the container should be restarted. For example, if the container exited with a failure error message, you could tell Azure to restart that container or simply ignore it and keep the container instance stopped. If you click Next, you have the Tags tab and then the Review + create.

After creating the container instance, you can open the resource and explore the options. On the Overview page, you have most of the details you'll need, such as IP address and FQDN, which you can use to access the application from the Web or a browser (in case it's a web application).

As you probably noticed, ACI is very straightforward. You ask for a container instance and you get one with an IP address. While very powerful, ACI is somewhat limited as mentioned earlier. For more flexibility, we have two other options as we'll see in the two final sections.

Windows Containers and Azure App Service

Azure App Service is one of Azure's Platform as a Service (PaaS) offerings. When using PaaS, you have to remember that the focus is on the application, not the infrastructure. With that said, App Service abstracts the server layer and allows you to focus on deploying and maintaining your web application. App Service provides a feature set to help you run and manage web applications, and in the case of containers, it provides an abstracted container host layer on which you just provide the image you want to run with your application and some details on the application itself, such as ports to open, and App Service does all the rest. From there, you can scale your application up or down and much more.

Just like the other services we're discussing in this chapter, App Service has a large number of functionalities to support web applications in different configurations and settings, different frameworks, on Windows and Linux, and so on. We'll be focusing on how we make a Windows container work on App Service. So, let's get started.

On the Azure Portal, you can navigate to the Create new resource option and type App Service. There will be multiple options, and the one we're looking for is the web app. When you select that option, you are presented with some details on what that offer is. Click Create. Next, you have the Basics tab (much like any other resource creation on Azure) as shown in Figure 6-9.

Figure 6-9. *Creating a new App Service web app*

The creation of our web app starts with regular Azure required information: what Subscription and Resource group to use. Next, we can provide a name for our instance, which is also used as the URL for our Web App. We then select which format we want the web app to use – either code or a Docker container. In our case, it's a Docker container, obviously. Next, we select Windows – App Service can't check the image type before it starts deploying, so in order to avoid installation errors, we should select the right option here. As every Azure resource, we can also select the region on which we're going to deploy our Web App. This information is important to ensure we are deploying the application close to our users to avoid latency issues. Finally, we have the App Service plan, which is used to configure the infrastructure to support the Web App, but also determines the cost of your solution on Azure. The pricing structure of App Service involves multiple factors, such as which type of environment you're deploying (dev/test, production, and isolated) and size of the VMs hosting your container/app using a concept called Azure Compute Unit (ACU). Going into the details on each plan is outside of the scope of this book, and I'd recommend you take a good look at the Azure documentation page to better understand which plan better fits your company's need.

On the next page, we have the details on the container image we want to use. The concept here is similar to what we saw in the "Windows Containers and Azure Container Instances" section. We can use Quickstart images, ACR, a Docker Hub registry, or a generic container registry. Depending on where you hosted your container image, you might choose a different option. Once you provided the correct information, you can click Next. On the Monitoring page, we have the option to integrate with Application Insights. At the moment of the writing of this book, the integration of Application Insights is not available for Windows Containers. To finalize the process, we have the Tags tab and the Review + create. If you are satisfied with the configuration, click Create.

You'll notice the deployment notification for the App Service web app finishes quite quickly. However, not everything is completed. When you open the Overview page of your App Service web app, you'll see the same URL you saw when you created the deployment. If you try to open, you'll see the message as shown in Figure 6-10.

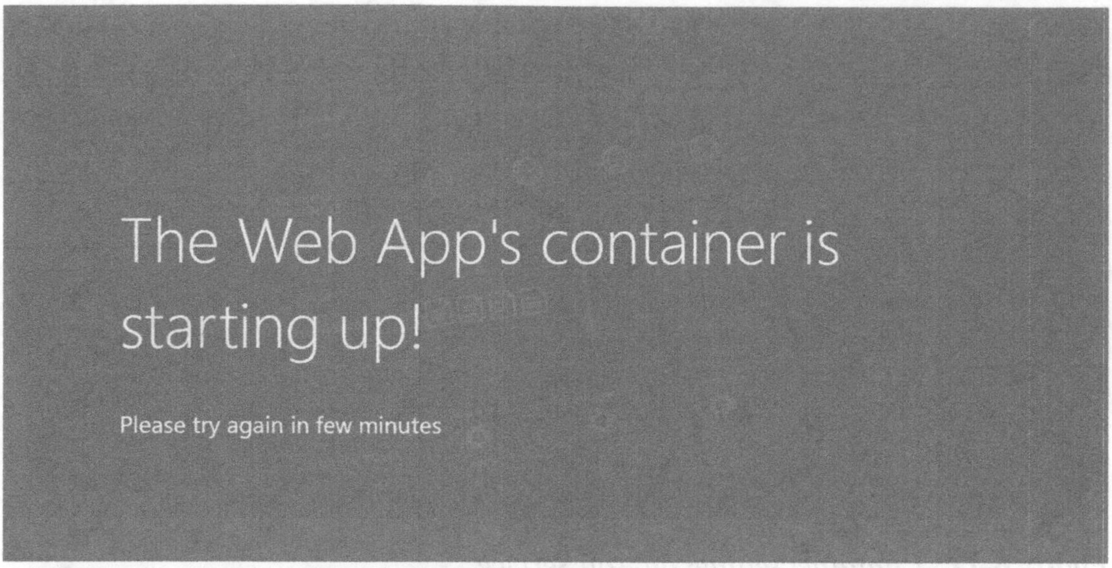

The Web App's container is starting up!

Please try again in few minutes

Figure 6-10. *Web App's container is starting up*

The process of deploying App Service is actually very interesting. The first thing Azure does is to put a temporary page to show your URL is up and running – even though the servers behind it are not ready. In the case of containers (especially Windows containers), it takes a while to pull the container images on the nodes supporting the web app. Let's take a look at some additional details on how App Service works.

First, on the Azure Portal, make sure you have the App Service web app open. Let's check the Container settings under Settings.

Figure 6-11.   *Container settings on App Service*

In this page, you can see the logs that App Service received from the containers on the hosts supporting the deployment of your application. Since the container might be coming from different sources, there are multiple options at the top – Azure Container Registry, Docker Hub, or Private Registry. Our deployment is using ACR, so you can see the details on the image we're using and the logs. One thing you'll notice here is that at first the logs will show that pull process. You'll see something like this:

```
18/09/2020 20:11:54.741 INFO - Site: ViniBeer - Image: vinibeerregistry.
azurecr.io/vinibeerwd:v6
Status: b4d4dcf61c8e Extracting
[>                                                 ]  262.1kB/25.8MB

18/09/2020 20:11:54.854 INFO - Site: ViniBeer - Image: vinibeerregistry.
azurecr.io/vinibeerwd:v6
Status: b4d4dcf61c8e Extracting
[===>                                              ]  1.573MB/25.8MB

18/09/2020 20:11:55.306 INFO - Site: ViniBeer - Image: vinibeerregistry.
azurecr.io/vinibeerwd:v6
Status: b4d4dcf61c8e Extracting
[====>                                             ]  2.359MB/25.8MB
```

```
18/09/2020 20:11:55.417 INFO - Site: ViniBeer - Image: vinibeerregistry.
azurecr.io/vinibeerwd:v6
Status: b4d4dcf61c8e Extracting
[=================>                              ]  8.389MB/25.8MB

18/09/2020 20:11:55.527 INFO - Site: ViniBeer - Image: vinibeerregistry.
azurecr.io/vinibeerwd:v6
Status: b4d4dcf61c8e Extracting
[==================>                             ]  9.699MB/25.8MB
```
Notice the progress bar shows the pull process happening until you get a message like

```
18/09/2020 20:12:01.195 INFO - Site: ViniBeer - Image: vinibeerregistry.
azurecr.io/vinibeerwd:v6
Status: b4d4dcf61c8e Pull complete
```

Then the logs will show the hosts finalizing the deployment process of the container, like Figure 6-11 shows. Once you reach that point, your web app will be up and running.

App Service does provide some other cool features that are totally automated. Let's look at some of them.

First, open the deployment Slots tab under Deployment. You'll notice we only have one slot. If you configured your App Service deployment like in this tutorial, you should see that it is your production slot. Slots on App Service will work as deployment environments on which you can deploy different versions of your web app. This comes in handy in a few situations:

- A/B testing: When you want a percentage of users accessing your website to see a different version than other users. This is traditionally used to test new features or to check how users react to a different configuration on your website.

- Production vs. development: Instead of simply replacing the production environment with a new version of the container, you can first create a new slot for the development version, try the website on the URL for that slot to ensure it works correctly, and then swap the slots.

Another interesting feature on App Service is the Scale options. There are two alternatives when you need to scale your application; you can either change the size of the hosts supporting your web app – that's Scale up and will take effect when you change the size of your App Service plan. The other option is Scale out – which means adding more instances of your container to run on more machines so your web app can support more users. To do that, navigate to Scale out (App Service plan) under Settings:

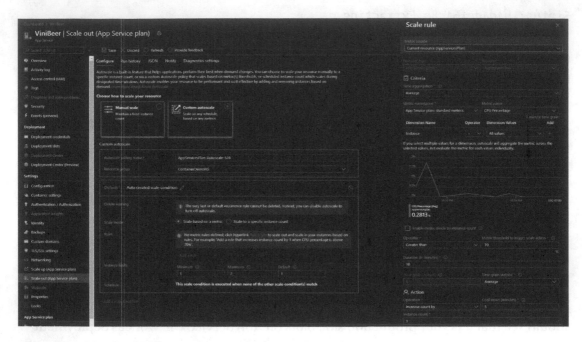

Figure 6-12. *Scale out option on App Service*

As you can see in Figure 6-12, there are multiple ways to set up the Scale out option. First, you can set up manually, which is a simple process of telling App Service how many instances of your container you want to run at the same time. You can manually add or remove instances. The other way is to set up a Custom autoscale rule. You can set up multiple rules, and they can be based on many factors: CPU, Memory, HTTP Queue, TCP Time Wait, and many other options. This granularity is great for making sure your users won't face a slow loading website when trying to access your application.

As you can see, App Service is a full-blown PaaS offer on Azure and works fine with Windows Containers. It provides an easier way to manage your application, so all you have to do is to ensure the app is running on the container and then maintain the deployment on App Service.

However, App Service is great for web applications. For other types of applications, we have another option to deploy Windows Containers – Azure Kubernetes Service.

Windows Containers and Azure Kubernetes Service

Before I get started on this topic, I want to bring up the warning I mentioned at the beginning of this chapter again: we're not covering everything on these services throughout this chapter. That is particularly true for Kubernetes and Azure Kubernetes Service (AKS).

Kubernetes (or K8s, for short) is a world on its own. Not only the platform evolved in the past few years, but also the ecosystem around it evolved a lot. We could have a book (a long one in fact) on Azure Kubernetes Service, just for Windows Containers (and I plan to write one, next). So, our goal here is to arm you with the minimal knowledge to get your AKS cluster up and running and deploy your first application using Windows Containers. With that said, let's cover some K8s basics.

K8s is an open source container orchestration platform. What that means is that its purpose is to manage the lifecycle of the container host and the containers and ensure high availability and load balance while taking care of components such as secrets, application specification, and much more. Its architecture is composed of several items, most notably the master and worker nodes. Let's cover some of the basics of each:

- Master node: Is responsible for running the brains of K8s. All services that need to connect to K8s do that through the master node. This is done via what is called Kubernetes APIs. The APIs serve as interface for two important services on the master node, the Controller Manager and Scheduler. Together, these two services ensure the desired state informed by the users is achieved by scheduling the nodes to run the containers necessary for the application. The most notable way to connect to K8s is via command line using a tool called kubectl. Also, while you may be using K8s to run Windows containers only, the master node has to be a Linux deployment.

- Worker node: Is responsible for running the containers that run the application. On K8s, containers run on what is called a pod. A pod can represent one or more containers. On each worker node, a process called kubelet is responsible for executing what the master node informed and scheduled for that node.

At the time of the writing of this book, there are conversations to change the term "master" on K8s in alignment with diversity and inclusion. Be aware that by the time you read this book, the term might have changed to something else.

Another important concept in K8s is that all deployments are made based on a desired state. What that means is that instead of going through a deployment process, you write the specification of your application on YAML file and K8s will try to match that specification on its environment. Here's how the process works (on a very high level):

1. You write a YAML file with the specification of how your application works.

2. Using kubectl, you open a connection to your K8s cluster and send a command to apply the specification on your YAML file.

3. The K8s master node will receive that instruction, and the Controller Manager will note the desired state is not in place and will start the process of deploying the pods. The Scheduler then assigns the worker nodes on which the pods will reside.

4. The worker nodes receive the notification from the master node that they should start running the containers to support the YAML file specification. K8s will also ensure a load balancer is in place in case you specified that in your YAML file.

5. If a change is made to the YAML file and applied again, K8s will check for the desire state again and will try to honor that change.

Interestingly though, the K8s services themselves also run on the same K8s mode. That's also true for services such as load balancer and specialized monitoring services. When you deploy K8s, you'll notice that there will be multiple containers already running in your cluster, even though you haven't deployed your apps yet. These containers are there to run the K8s infrastructure itself.

With all this said, let's take a look at how AKS works by deploying a new AKS cluster. On the Azure Portal, open the Create a resource menu and type Kubernetes Service. Select the Kubernetes Service option and then click the Create button on the Overview page.

The AKS cluster creation wizard starts like many other deployments on Azure, asking which Subscription and Resource group to use. Then we have the Kubernetes cluster name which will be used for administrative tasks only. Next, we have region, which is also a point you should consider in terms of latency between the service (AKS cluster) and the users accessing the applications on top of it. The Kubernetes version is also an important aspect as it defines which K8s features will be available. It is also important to note that Windows containers themselves became generally available (GA) on K8s, version 1.14, and on AKS, version 1.15. Since these are older releases and are no longer available on AKS, you can choose any version, and they will support Windows Containers. Still, if you have special requirements on K8s (for customers using K8s already), you might want to check the support matrix on the documentation page and the K8s change log available at `https://github.com/kubernetes/kubernetes/blob/master/CHANGELOG/README.md`.

Next (still on the Basics tab), we have the configuration of the primary node pool. Here let me pause and explain one thing: given the architecture mentioned earlier, AKS is a cloud service that abstracts part of the infrastructure necessary to run K8s. It abstracts the master node, so you only need to take care of the worker nodes. These worker nodes are regular Azure VMs that AKS will configure to run your containers. In fact, that's how Azure charges AKS. There are no AKS-related costs, only Azure VMs. With that said, AKS still needs a Linux primary node pool. You can then create new node pools with Windows nodes for the Windows workloads. Here we can select the size of the VMs to support the primary (Linux) node pool. If you don't plan to run any workloads on this node pool, you can leave the default size. The node count is also dependent on the workloads you want to run and how many replicas. Depending on that, you might need more or less nodes. Once you are satisfied with the options here, you can click Next to check the Node pools tab.

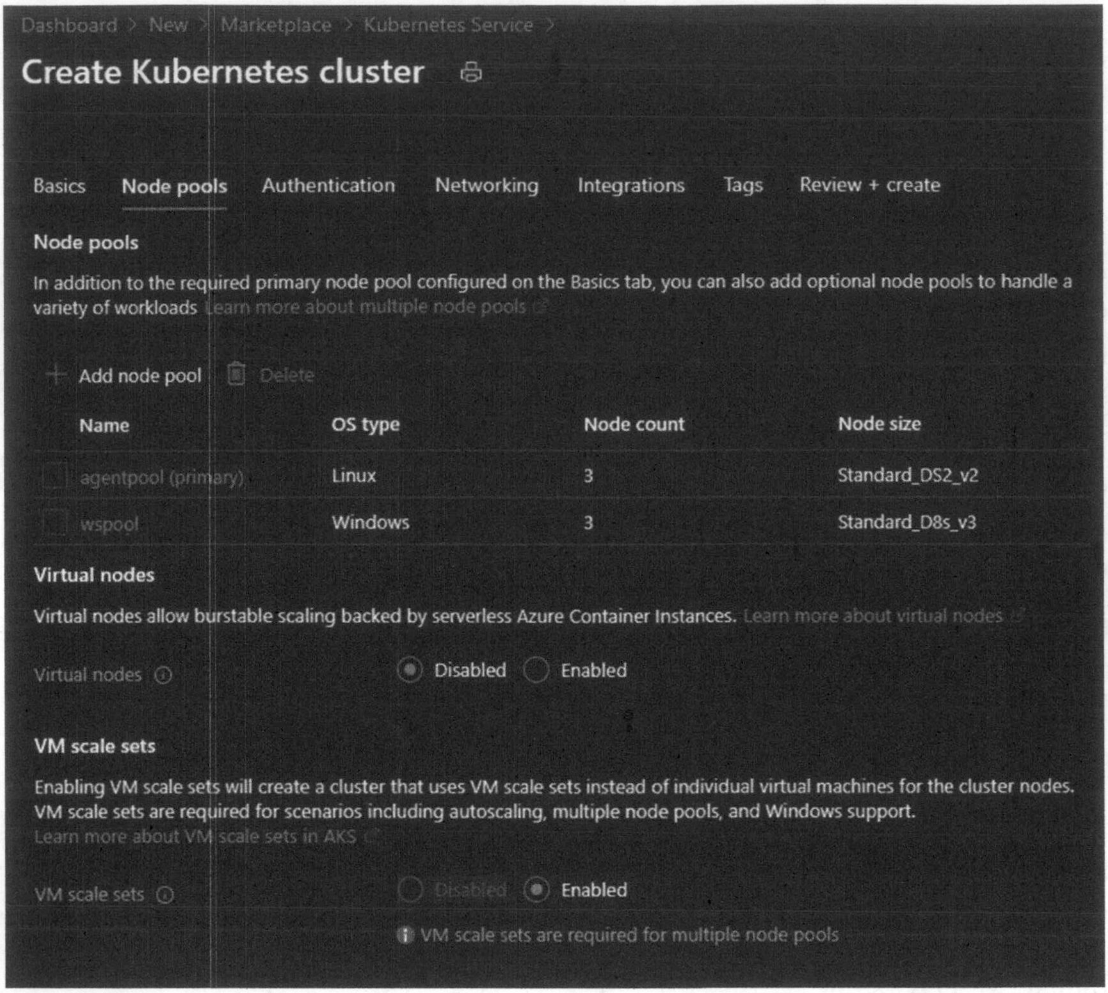

Figure 6-13. *Node pools configuration on AKS cluster creation wizard*

The Node pools tab is where we define how the Windows nodes will work. By default, you'll see only the primary node pool from the previous page. Here you can add a new node pool. You can provide a node pool name, which OS you want for that node pool (Windows in our case), the size of the VMs in that node pool, and how many nodes supporting that node pool. As you can see in Figure 6-13, I created a new wspool for my Windows nodes, with a node count of 3 VMs and with a larger VM size than the primary node pool.

Next, we have the option to enable Virtual nodes, which uses ACI to run containers in the background. This is a good way to quickly scale your container count without having to create new VMs on your AKS cluster. Finally, we have the VM Scale sets, which we covered in the first section of this chapter for Azure VMs. The principle here is the same. AKS will create the VMs on a Scale set so it can then scale up or down the number of VMs. For Windows nodes, using Scale sets is also a requirement. Click Next to get to the Authentication tab.

Here we have an important configuration on your AKS cluster. The authentication method chosen here will be used by the AKS service to manage other cloud resources attached to your cluster. For example, your AKS cluster is composed of container hosts (nodes on the K8s nomenclature) that need to authenticate against your registry on Azure Container Registry. On a high level, both options are essentially an Azure Active Directory identity used to authenticate a service. However, the Managed Identity option does not require that you manage the identity manually. If you have a compliance or security requirement to use a specific service principal, make sure you follow that. Otherwise, Managed Identities do offer some flexibility and less management overhead. In addition to that, if you decide to use a service principal, you need to manually configure the other resources to allow your AKS cluster to access it. This configuration is outside the scope of this book. Still on the Authentication tab, we have the option to set up how you want to authenticate and authorize users in your AKS cluster and the encryption type for VM disks.

Next we have the Networking tab. Networking on Kubernetes is another topic that requires a long explanation. To simplify, for Windows containers, the only option available is to configure an Azure virtual network to be used by the VMs on your AKS cluster. To do that, you need to select the Advanced option and then configure which virtual network to use or create a new one. In addition, you have other network settings such as DNS prefix (used as FQDN).

On the Integrations tab, we can start configuring other Azure services for use with your AKS cluster. First, we have the registry with ACR. If you selected System-wide Managed Identity back in the Authentication tab, you'll be able to select which registry to integrate. You can also configure Azure monitoring to provide monitoring services to your cluster and containers and Azure Policy to apply centralized configurations. Finally, we have the Tags and Review + create tabs. Click Create to start deploying your AKS cluster. This process might take several minutes to complete.

When the deployment completes, you can navigate to the resource. There are a bunch of settings to look at on AKS. Let's start by looking at the Node pools, as shown in Figure 6-14.

Figure 6-14. *Node pools configuration on AKS*

In this tab, you can see the node pools we created on the deployment of our AKS cluster. Here you can create a new node pool – in case you want to segregate the workloads on different hosts. You can also set the scale method for each node pool. You can set for Manual scale or Autoscale. On Autoscale, AKS will monitor the resources available and the ability of the K8s master node to schedule containers and pods and make decisions to add or remove nodes depending on the workload.

Next, let's look at the Insights tab.

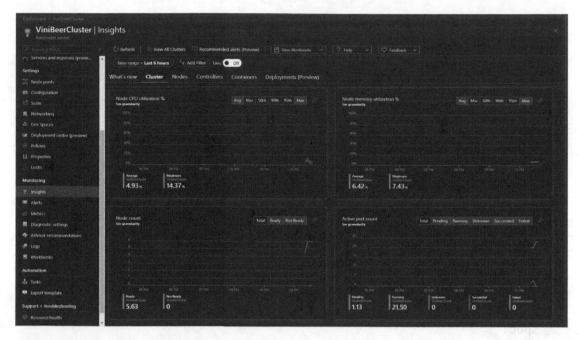

Figure 6-15. *Azure Insights on AKS*

Here we have something that I personally enjoy: embedded management for the AKS cluster and containers. As you can see in Figure 6-15, as soon as the cluster is up and running, we have metrics to monitor the state of it. Also note in the same figure that we have management at node level, controller level, container level, or deployment level. We'll come back to this page later to see our workload deployed. Now let's see how we actually get our application deployed to AKS.

As I explained previously, deploying a workload on K8s requires that you have a YAML file specification to describe how your application works. The AKS documentation page provides a sample YAML file that you can use to get started. For our demonstration, I prepared a YAML file based on the preceding sample and modified it to deploy my ViniBeer application from the container we created earlier in this book. It's a nice way to close the cycle all the way back from an old server to now AKS. You can find this YAML file I'll be using in this example in my GitHub page at `https://github.com/vrapolinario/AKSDemo/blob/master/vinibeer.yaml`.

Here's the content of that YAML file:

```yaml
apiVersion: apps/v1
kind: Deployment
metadata:
  name: vinibeer
  labels:
    app: vinibeer
spec:
  replicas: 3
  template:
    metadata:
      name: vinibeer
      labels:
        app: vinibeer
    spec:
      nodeSelector:
        "beta.kubernetes.io/os": windows
      containers:
      - name: vinibeer
        image: viniapregistry.azurecr.io/vinibeerimage:v1
        resources:
          limits:
            cpu: 1
            memory: 800M
          requests:
            cpu: .1
            memory: 300M
        ports:
          - containerPort: 80
  selector:
    matchLabels:
      app: vinibeer
---
apiVersion: v1
kind: Service
```

```
metadata:
  name: vinibeer
spec:
  type: LoadBalancer
  ports:
  - protocol: TCP
    port: 80
  selector:
    app: vinibeer
```

I know the preceding code might be a lot to digest at first, so let's look at it in detail. First, notice that we have two main blocks of code defined by the kind: deployment and service.

If you are not familiar with any programing language or code, a good way to identify blocks of code is to look at the alignment of the code structure. In the preceding example, note that each block starts aligned most to the left-hand side and the code that belongs to that block is aligned one point to the right on each new set of information.

What the presence of the preceding two blocks on the YAML file means is that K8s has two things to look at: a deployment, which is used to (as the name says) deploy a container/pod, and a service, which will work as the load balancer on this case. Now let's look at each component.

First, you might have noticed that both blocks actually started by stating which API version of K8s to use. This is future-looking feature since K8s only has one version (as of the writing of this book), but in the future, there might be more than one and they might not be compatible in terms and features, so this option says which version to use. Next, we have the kind term that we briefly covered. There are more kinds to be used but we won't cover in this book.

Then we have some metadata information that will be used by K8s to identify your application. Next, we have the spec for the deployment kind. Since the deployment here is a container, you'll see that we have some container-related information, such as which container image to use, what type of node to use for this container image, how much CPU and memory we are requesting and limiting for this container, and the container port. We are also stating that this spec should match the label for our application. One important aspect of the spec for the deployment is the replica count. This is how you tell K8s how many containers/pods you'd like to have hosting your application.

Moving on in the YAML file, we have the next set of block of code – the service. As you can see, the API version is also v1, and we also have some metadata. This kind also has a spec configuration, but in the case of service, we have the type, which in our case is Load Balancer (written all together), and the ports to be open with its protocol.

There is an infinite number of combinations and a vast set of configurations and options that are possible to use here. I recommend that you take a look at the K8s documentation to learn more about authoring a YAML file for K8s. The documentation is available here: `https://kubernetes.io/docs/home/`. For now, save the preceding code (from GitHub) as a YAML file on your machine. Give it a name such as ViniBeer.yaml.

With this YAML file, we can now start the deployment of our application on our AKS cluster. But in order to do that, we need to connect to the cluster. I mentioned previously that the most common way to connect to a K8s cluster is via kubectl, and AKS makes that process easier. Simply navigate to the Overview page and click Connect.

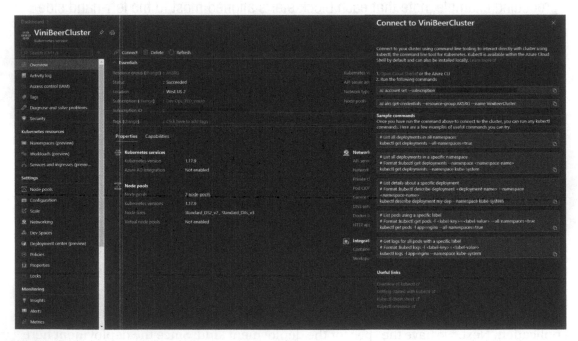

Figure 6-16. *Connecting to your AKS cluster*

The simplest way to start the connection to your AKS cluster is to open the Azure Cloud Shell link as shown in Figure 6-16. This will open a new tab and create a Cloud Shell connection to your Azure account. Then you can run the two commands shown also in Figure 6-16 to connect that Azure Cloud Shell session to your AKS cluster using kubectl. Kubectl is already available on Azure Cloud Shell, so there's no additional configuration other than the preceding commands. If you want to, you can also download kubectl manually to your machine and manually configure the connection. In our case, we'll use the Azure Cloud Shell. This is the output from the preceding commands:

```
PS /home/vinicius> az account set --subscription <My Subscription ID>
PS /home/vinicius> az aks get-credentials --resource-group AKSRG --name
ViniBeerCluster
Merged "ViniBeerCluster" as current context in /home/vinicius/.kube/config
```

Notice that Azure Cloud Shell saved the kubectl config file on the preceding folder. To better understand this, Azure Cloud Shell is not using the storage on your machine. Rather, it uses an Azure storage account to manage files. The nice thing here is that if you decide to use kubectl on your machine, you can simply copy this file over. In fact, for the next step, we'll need to upload our YAML file.

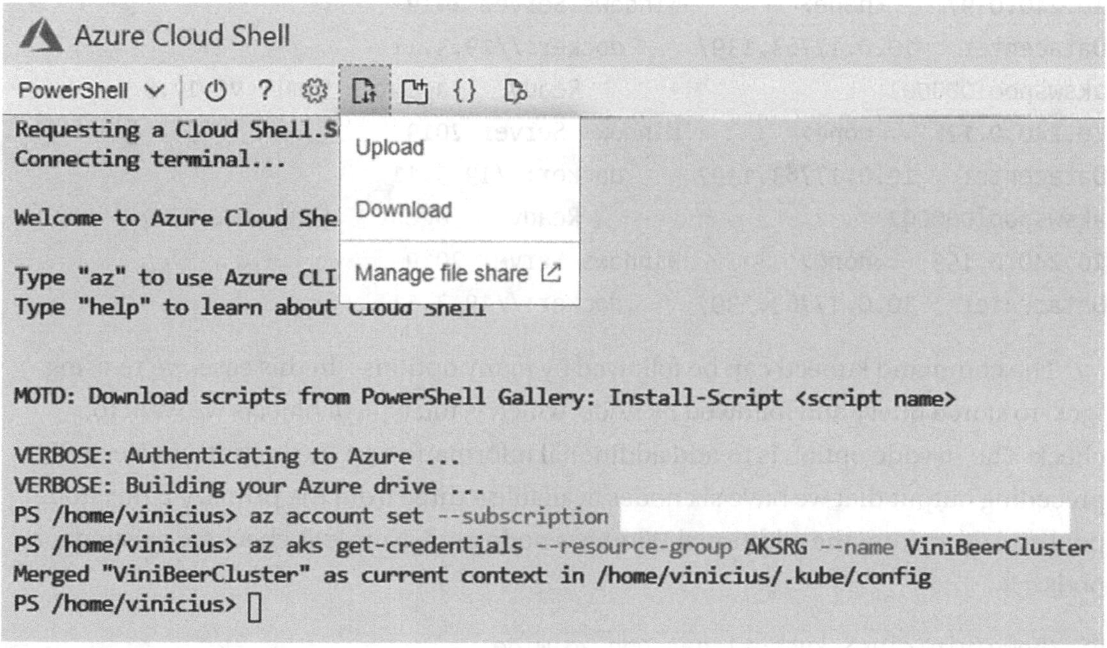

Figure 6-17. *Upload a file to Azure Cloud Shell*

Once you click Upload as shown in Figure 6-17, you can select a file from your computer. Select the file you saved before (ViniBeer.yaml). A message on the footnote will let you know once the upload completes. Now, let's start exploring kubectl.

First, let's see our nodes:

```
PS /home/vinicius> kubectl get node -o wide
NAME                               STATUS    ROLES   AGE    VERSION
INTERNAL-IP     EXTERNAL-IP    OS-IMAGE                        KERNEL-
VERSION        CONTAINER-RUNTIME
aks-agentpool-15807463-vmss000000  Ready     agent   53m    v1.17.9
10.240.0.4      <none>         Ubuntu 16.04.7
LTS              4.15.0-1092-azure   docker://19.3.12
aks-agentpool-15807463-vmss000001  Ready     agent   53m    v1.17.9
10.240.0.35     <none>         Ubuntu 16.04.7
LTS              4.15.0-1092-azure   docker://19.3.12
aks-agentpool-15807463-vmss000002  Ready     agent   53m    v1.17.9
10.240.0.66     <none>         Ubuntu 16.04.7
LTS              4.15.0-1092-azure   docker://19.3.12
akswspool000000                    Ready     agent   51m    v1.17.9
10.240.0.97     <none>         Windows Server 2019
Datacenter    10.0.17763.1397     docker://19.3.11
akswspool000001                    Ready     agent   51m    v1.17.9
10.240.0.128    <none>         Windows Server 2019
Datacenter    10.0.17763.1397     docker://19.3.11
akswspool000002                    Ready     agent   51m    v1.17.9
10.240.0.159    <none>         Windows Server 2019
Datacenter    10.0.17763.1397     docker://19.3.11
```

The command kubectl can be followed by many options – in this case, we're using "get" to start a query and followed by node, which is the type of objects we want to check. The -o wide option is to add additional information on the output. Notice on the preceding output that we have six nodes available – three from the primary Linux node pool and three from the additional Windows node pool. Now let's check for existing pods:

```
PS /home/vinicius> kubectl get pod -o wide
No resources found in default namespace.
```

The preceding command queries for existing pods, but since we haven't deployed any, there's nothing to show.

You can also run the preceding same command, but add -A to the end. That will show all containers on all namespaces. Namespaces are a way to separate workloads on the same cluster in case you have many users and different workloads and projects. The result of the preceding command with the addition of -A would also show the containers that are actually running the K8s infrastructure.

We can also check for existing deployments:

```
PS /home/vinicius> kubectl get deployment -o wide
No resources found in default namespace.
```

And we can also check for services:

NAME	TYPE	CLUSTER-IP	EXTERNAL-IP	PORT(S)	AGE	SELECTOR
kubernetes	ClusterIP	10.0.0.1	<none>	443/TCP	60m	<none>

In the preceding text, you can see that the only existing service is the default K8s service that supports the cluster itself.

Now let's deploy our application. Make sure you are on the same folder context as you uploaded your file:

```
PS /home/vinicius> dir

    Directory: /home/vinicius

Mode                 LastWriteTime         Length Name
----                 -------------         ------ ----
-----           9/22/2020 6:13 AM            803 ViniBeer.yaml
PS /home/vinicius> kubectl apply -f ViniBeer.yaml
deployment.apps/vinibeer created
service/vinibeer created
```

In the preceding code, we first checked for the file we wanted to deploy (ViniBeer.yaml), and then we used the kubectl apply command to tell AKS to apply the specification of that file, represented by -f and the file name. The result is the initialization of the deployment and the service.

Now let's check the same items we checked in the preceding code:

```
PS /home/vinicius> kubectl get deployment -o wide
NAME        READY   UP-TO-DATE   AVAILABLE   AGE    CONTAINERS
IMAGES                                       SELECTOR
vinibeer    0/3     3            0           16s    vinibeer
viniapregistry.azurecr.io/vinibeerimage:v1    app=vinibeer
PS /home/vinicius> kubectl get services -o wide
NAME         TYPE            CLUSTER-IP    EXTERNAL-IP     PORT(S)
AGE     SELECTOR
kubernetes   ClusterIP       10.0.0.1      <none>          443/TCP
73m     <none>
vinibeer     LoadBalancer    10.0.95.9     51.143.106.56   80:32582/
TCP     23s     app=vinibeer
PS /home/vinicius> kubectl get pod -o wide
NAME                         READY   STATUS             RESTARTS   AGE
IP        NODE               NOMINATED NODE   READINESS GATES
vinibeer-78488449cc-lkww2    0/1     ContainerCreating  0          29s
<none>    akswspool000002    <none>              <none>
vinibeer-78488449cc-rcv6l    0/1     ContainerCreating  0          29s
<none>    akswspool000001    <none>              <none>
vinibeer-78488449cc-tmwnq    0/1     ContainerCreating  0          29s
<none>    akswspool000000    <none>              <none>
```

As you can see, we ran the same commands to check the deployment, the service, and the pods. The deployment shows our deployment of the ViniBeer application (as in the metadata) with a total number of 0 of 3 ready, based on YAML file's replica count for the deployment. The reason it is showing 0 of 3 ready is because the containers are being created and the nodes have to pull the images.

Next, we see the service, which was quickly created. We have it shown as LoadBalancer as expected, and we also have the external IP address that will be used to access the application later.

Finally, we have the pods. Notice that all pods are showing with the status of "ContainerCreating" as explained earlier. Also note the name of the nodes. It reflects the node pool name of our Windows node pool, because we specified in the YAML file to use Windows nodes. After waiting for the pods to deploy, you can run the same command again, and it now should show as running:

```
PS /home/vinicius> kubectl get pod -o wide
NAME                            READY   STATUS    RESTARTS   AGE
IP               NODE           NOMINATED NODE   READINESS GATES
vinibeer-78488449cc-1kww2   1/1     Running    0              6m49s
10.240.0.170   akswspool000002   <none>          <none>
vinibeer-78488449cc-rcv6l   1/1     Running    0              6m49s
10.240.0.153   akswspool000001   <none>          <none>
vinibeer-78488449cc-tmwnq   1/1     Running    0              6m49s
10.240.0.101   akswspool000000   <none>          <none>
```

Let's get the IP address from the service and try to access the application.

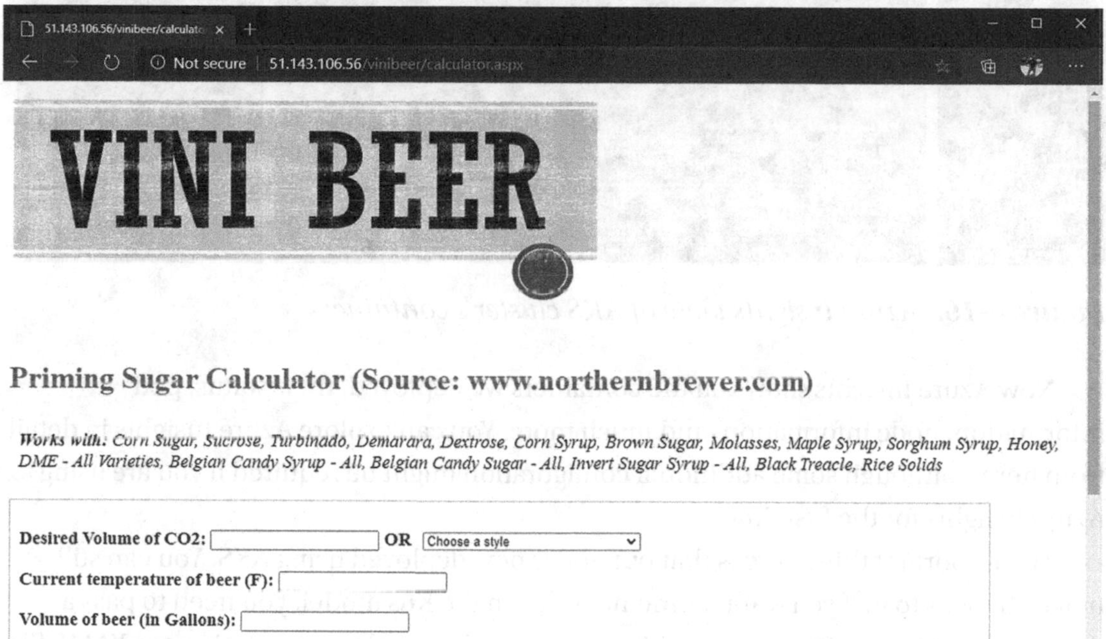

Figure 6-18. *ViniBeer application running on AKS*

As you can see in Figure 6-18, the IP address we're using to access the application is the same as the one we got from the output of the service earlier. Our application is now up and running on AKS with the container image we used back in Chapter 3.

To close our tour on AKS, let's go back to the Azure Portal and look at the Insights page again, now at the Containers tab, as showin in Figure 6-19.

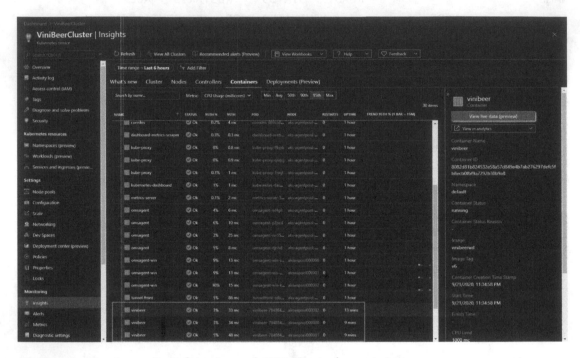

Figure 6-19. *Azure Insights view of AKS cluster's containers*

Now Azure Insights shows all the containers we deployed, their status, pod information, node information, and much more. You can explore Azure Insights in detail from here – although some additional configuration might be required if you are using Azure Insights for the first time.

The important thing here is that our app is now deployed using AKS. You can still make changes to it, if you want. Remember that in the K8s model, you need to pass a desired state to your K8s cluster, so all you need to do is make a change in your YAML file and run the same apply command again, for example, if I change the YAML file to have four replicas of my containers and run the apply command again:

```
PS /home/vinicius> kubectl apply -f ViniBeer.yaml
deployment.apps/vinibeer configured
```

```
service/vinibeer unchanged
PS /home/vinicius> kubectl get pod -o wide
NAME                          READY   STATUS                    RESTARTS   AGE
IP              NODE                   NOMINATED NODE   READINESS GATES
vinibeer-78488449cc-lkww2     1/1     Running                   0          22m
10.240.0.170    akswspool000002   <none>              <none>
vinibeer-78488449cc-rcv6l     1/1     Running                   0          22m
10.240.0.153    akswspool000001   <none>              <none>
vinibeer-78488449cc-sv8sl     0/1     ContainerCreating  0          5s
<none>          akswspool000000   <none>              <none>
vinibeer-78488449cc-tmwnq     1/1     Running                   0          22m
10.240.0.101    akswspool000000   <none>              <none>
```

Notice the preceding first command is the same as before. The output shows the service is unchanged, but the deployment is now configured with the new parameter of four replicas. This is reflected in the next command on which we show the pods, and we see a new container coming up.

All is good with our Windows Container application on AKS!

Conclusion

What a journey, right? I sincerely hope you enjoyed reading this book. More importantly, I hope this book opened your eyes on how the container technology can help even IT admins, IT Pros, and Ops folks with their environments and workloads.

Containers allow for greater simplification of the infrastructure, by reducing the virtualization overhead, but that comes with the price of learning something new. And we covered a lot of ground! From understanding what the technology is, what Docker is and how it plays in the container ecosystem, what the architecture of containers looks like, and which scenarios to use to how Windows containers compare to Linux. We looked at some containers basics, such as how to deploy a container host, how to run your first containers, and what a docker file is.

Since Windows Containers have a great appeal to modernizing legacy workloads, we looked at how to containerize an existing application; how to enable your Windows container to work with existing infrastructure, such as Active Directory, devices, and GPU; and even some best practices so you don't fall into any container trap.

Then we dived deep into the weeds of managing resources for Windows containers, for CPU and memory, the importance of storage for containers when you need persistent storage, networking configurations so your containers can communicate with the outside world correctly, and so on.

We also looked at Windows Admin Center and how it greatly simplifies the job of managing containers, creating new container images, connecting to Azure Container Registry, and more. And speaking of Azure services, we topped it all with this chapter in which we covered Azure services on which you can run your containers with VMs, registry, instances, App Service, and AKS! Wow! What a long list!

I hope you feel this content enriched your tech knowledge and that you feel you can now take on the challenge to work on a project with Windows Containers!

Here's my vote of good luck!

You can find me on Twitter (@vrapolinario).

Index

A

Access Control List (ACL), 117, 162
Access to devices, 77, 78
Active Directory (AD)
  gMSA
    console applications, 76
    preceding command, 74
    running containers, 76, 77
    web applications, 75
    Windows service apps, 76
Anti-virus (AV) containers, 81
Application programing interface (API), 6
App Service
  container settings, 190
  deploy, 189
  Scale options, 192
  web app, 191
Azure CLI and Azure PowerShell, 168
Azure Cloud Shell, 168, 203
Azure Compute Unit (ACU), 188
Azure Container Instance (ACI), 183
  create new container, 184
  options, 185
Azure Container Registry (ACR), 169
  access keys management, 171
  checking image, 175
  creation basics, 169
  docker login command, 172
  pulling container image, 176
  push command, 173, 174
  SKU feature, 170
Azure Hybrid Benefit (AHB), 29
Azure Kubernetes Service (AKS), 193
  Azure Insights, 199
  Cloud Shell, 203
  cluster containers, 208
  cluster creation, 195–197
  connecting cluster, 202
  networking, 197
  node pools, 198
  nodes, 193
  process, 194
  YAML file, 201, 202
Azure Portal, 168, 169, 171, 177, 183, 185

B

Back up containers, 80, 81
Brand-new container image, 49

C

Classless Inter-Domain
    Routing (CIDR), 123
Cloud Shell connection, 203
Command-line interface (CLI), 15, 168
Command Prompt (CMD), 6, 14, 15, 31
Container
  CLI, 15

© Vinicius Ramos Apolinario 2021
V. Ramos Apolinario, *Windows Containers for IT Pros*, https://doi.org/10.1007/978-1-4842-6686-1

Printed in the United States
By Bookmasters